Girl Baby Names for 2(

Girl Baby Names for 2017

Hannah Crawford

ISBN:1537787896

ISBN-13: 978-1537787893

Penguinies@outlook.com

DEDICATED

This book is dedicated to my two gorgeous little boys Troy and Jemai. I would also like to dedicate this book to Bradley for blessing me with my second son. I love you all with the whole of my heart, always & forever.

Introduction

The Girl Baby Names for 2017 book has over 1700 first names to help you to decide on the right name for your baby. There is a wide variety to choose from with both modern and classic names listed alphabetically. With pronunciations, origins and meanings all included to give you a better understanding of each name.

The Girl Baby Names for 2017 book can help you to pick a suitable baby name that suits your child and family surname. Each name has been divided up into easily readable sections. Agreeing on a special baby name can be one of the most difficult yet rewarding decisions that any parent can make during their lifetime. This book can help make choosing a baby name easy and lots of fun.

Contents

Girl Baby Names for 2017

How to choose a baby name

Finding out that you are expecting a baby is one of the most joyous and happiest moments that you can experience in your life. Some parents already have name choices and know what they want to call their baby long before they find out that they are pregnant, however, for others, this can be a daunting and difficult task.

I know when I was expecting my first son I found it extremely difficult to pick a name that I thought would be perfect for him, and a couple of months before he was born, I finally settled on a name. However, once my son was born and I held him in my arms for the first time, I quickly realised the name that I had spent so many months deciding on didn't seem to suit him and I was back to square one.

Names are a part of everyday life and culture; they can have a great significance to the child who receives the name and also to the societies that give them. A baby name is not only a name that will be with your infant throughout its childhood; it is a name that will stick with them for life. To add to the pressure, there is such a huge range and variety of baby names to choose from and to consider that the task can seem tremendously overwhelming. The Girl Baby Names for 2017 *book* has suggested a few helpful tips when it comes to choosing a baby name that is right for you, your child and family.

Where to start

Decide what are the most important factors for you and your partner when choosing a baby name; this may include any family traditions, uniqueness, popularity, celebrity influences, or gender.

It is a good idea to make a list of your favourite baby names and share them with your partner who can do the same with you. Combine your favourite names into one list and use this as a starting point. If you do not have a partner, you could make a list with a good friend or a family member and have lots of fun listening to each other's name suggestions. You can add more names along the way; no doubt you will have lots of name suggestions from family members, friends and even from strangers that you can also add to your list of possible baby names.

One popular choice for parents-to-be is to name their newborn baby after a grandparent, relative or an ancestor. Your baby's heritage will always be an essential aspect of who they are as an individual. Choosing a name that is important to you or your family can reflect this. Some families have a strict naming tradition that dates back generations. Although you should never let anybody pressure you into naming your baby something that you are not keen on or do not really like. Instead, you could consider using them as middle names to honour your family traditions. This can make the process a whole lot simpler. However, this choice is not for everybody, for me personally this was not an option.

Unique names

For some parents one of the most important aspects when deciding on a name for their baby is the uniqueness of it. The obvious advantage in choosing a unique or unusual baby name is how it can stand out from the crowd and be remembered throughout time. Some people like the shock factor that a unique name can generate for the child. The downside of picking a unique or unusual name is pronunciation; numerous people may struggle to pronounce your child's name which could bring negative attention to your child for all of the wrong reasons. The name may be hard for others to spell and constantly having to correct people who cannot spell or pronounce the name can become tiring, especially for your child when he/she is at school.

Choosing a unique baby name can allow the parents to use and to also show off their own personal creativity. This could be a lot of fun, albeit if you choose this option, you should prepare yourself for being asked numerous questions about your chosen baby name and the reasons behind it. Modern celebrities often pick unusual and unique names for their babies which can generate a lot of publicity for them and their new-born child. Another thing to consider if you are looking for a unique baby name is that the name may sound cute and adorable when the baby is young, although when the child grows up into an adult, the name could possibly sound outrageous and somewhat ridiculous. Some parents might feel too embarrassed to consider using a unique baby name for their child and may prefer to opt for a more traditional name instead.

A rising trend with parents who are opting to pick unique baby names for their children is for them to use names that begin with or have the letter 'x' in them. The reason being that the names are thought to have a unique and edgy style and sound over other baby names. Angelina Jolie facilitated this popularisation by choosing names that had the letter 'x' in them for three of her five children, Pax, Maddox, and Knox.

Girl Baby Names for 2017

Boys Names with the letter X

1. Alexander
2. Axel
3. Baxter
4. Braxton
5. Bronx
6. Dixon
7. Felix
8. Huxley
9. Jax
10. Lennox
11. Madox
12. Maxim
13. Maxwell
14. Pax
15. Rex

Girls Names with the letter X

1. Alexa
2. Alexandra
3. Alexis
4. Beatrix
5. Dixie
6. Exene
7. Jaxine
8. Moxie
9. Oxsana
10. Phoenix
11. Roxanne
12. Trixie
13. Xena
14. Xenia
15. Xiomara

Name meanings and connotations

Name meanings can be an important attribute to a family when considering a baby name. Some names have different meanings in different cultures and countries that have evolved from different languages, this can be a little confusing when deciding on a baby name. However, it can also be a positive as the meaning of the name may be more desirable in one culture than it is in another.

Some names may have personal connotations, even though your partner may love one name it might remind you of somebody that you don't get along with, or it could be the same name as an ex-partner or ex-friend, etc. You may have found a perfect name that you have always loved and wanted to give to your newborn baby however a friend or family member may have got there first and used the same name for their child. This might put you off from using the name for your own baby. Alternatively, you may love the name so much that you might decide to give the name to your baby anyway.

Pronunciation and sound

How to pronounce your baby's name and how it sounds when spoken aloud is often an essential element to all parents when choosing a name for their baby. A name could sound harmonious and pleasant, alternatively, it may sound harsh or brash which could be an ultimate decision maker. The name could also be extremely difficult for others to pronounce which could end up completely changing your opinion on the name.

Surnames

Considering your child's surname is a common practice for a lot of parents when choosing a baby name as it can help you to pick the right name. Some parents prefer to avoid names that rhyme with their surnames while others favour this option. Names that flow with your baby's last surname can help you to narrow your list down. People can be ever so cruel when it comes to nicknames which are usually given to a person during their adolescent years. This is something that you could consider when choosing a name for your baby, especially when it comes to the initials. Check what the initials spell out, for example, Georgina Imogen Thomas sounds like a nice name. However, the initials are somewhat unfortunate in what they spell out. This is something that could be picked up on by classmates, family members, work colleagues and even by strangers. This could be rather embarrassing and unpleasant for your child to have to experience throughout their life.

Can you agree on a name?

One of the reasons why choosing a baby name can become so difficult for a lot of parents is because it's a decision that both you and your partner often make together. Finding a name that two people like can be tricky and take a lot longer than if it was just one person who was making the decision on their own. However, if your partner strongly disagrees with one of your favourite choice names you should listen to their opinions and not force a name that isn't liked or appreciated by both sides as it can cause conflict and resentment. If you both make a list of favourite baby names you can look through each other's lists and then discuss the pros and cons of each one, this could help the process dramatically. Your partner may have some really great ideas for names that you hadn't thought about before. Therefore, it's always good to share your honest thoughts and opinions with one and other.

Does the name suit your baby?

As I mentioned previously, I spent months looking through and researching baby names until I found one that I thought would be perfect for my son just before he was born. When I finally decided on a name that I thought would be ideal for my child I was a hundred percent sure that this was going to be his name for life. However, as soon as my son arrived into this world I quickly realised that the name that I was so certain about before did not suit him or his little personality at all. We spent the next few days thinking up alternative names until we found the perfect one that did suit him to the T. Luckily you are given 42 days after your baby is born to register the name officially in England, Wales and Northern Ireland. This means you could try out alternative names and see which one best suits him/her before you make your final decision.

Name popularity

Names that are already extremely popular and are in the top ten can be a decision maker when deciding on a baby name. Some parents like to pick a popular baby name, while others prefer to choose a name that is out of the top ten or even the top hundred baby names category. Celebrities can also have a drastic effect on the popularisation of a baby name. The name Harper has seen the largest rise in girls' names; this is most likely due to the celebrity couple Victoria and David Beckham who chose the name for their daughter in 2011. The name Eric rose by 314% in 2014 after celebrity Simon Cowell chose it for his first born son.

The media can also have a huge influence in popularising baby names in addition to celebrities. The popular television series, Game of Thrones has recently inspired some parents with their choice of baby names particularly, those who gave birth to baby girls. Almost two hundred and fifty babies have been named Arya, and fifty-three babies have been named Khaleesi. Although the male names have proven to be less influential, they have still been rather popular with eighteen babies being called Theon and seventeen babies named Tyrion.

Likewise, the release of a new Disney movie always tends to influence people's choices in baby names. Recently there has been a dramatic rise in babies being named Elsa, which was the name used for the Ice Queen in the animated blockbuster 2013 film Frozen.

Popular Baby Names in Regions within England

Region	Girls	Boys
East	Olivia	Oliver
East Midlands	Olivia	Oliver
West Midlands	Amelia	Muhammad
North East	Amelia	Oliver
North West	Amelia	Oliver
Yorkshire & The Humber	Amelia	Oliver
London	Amelia	Muhammad
South East	Amelia	Oliver
South West	Amelia	Oliver

The Top Baby Names in England

Girls	Boys
1. Amelia	1. Oliver
2. Olivia	2. Jack
3. Emily	3. Harry
4. Isla	4. George
5. Ava	5. Jacob
6. Ella	6. Charlie
7. Jessica	7. Noah
8. Isabella	8. William
9. Mia	9. Thomas
10. Poppy	10. Oscar

The Top Baby Names in Wales

Girls	Boys
1. Amelia	1. Oliver
2. Olivia	2. Jacob
3. Ava	3. Charlie
4. Isla	4. Jack
5. Emily	5. Noah
6. Ella	6. Alfie
7. Mia	7. Oscar
8. Isabella	8. William
9. Lilly	9. George
10. Evie	10. Harry

The Top Baby Names in Scotland

Girls	Boys
1. Emily	1. Jack
2. Sophie	2. Oliver
3. Olivia	3. James
4. Isla	4. Lewis
5. Ava	5. Alexander
6. Jessica	6. Charlie
7. Amelia	7. Logan
8. Ella	8. Lucas
9. Lucy	9. Harris
10. Lily	10. Daniel

The Top Baby Names in Northern Ireland

Girls	Boys
1. Emily	1. James
2. Ella	2. Jack
3. Grace	3. Noah
4. Sophie	4. Charlie
5. Olivia	5. Daniel
6. Anna	6. Oliver
7. Amelia	7. Matthew
8. Aoife	8. Harry
9. Lucy	9. Tomas
10. Ava	10. Jake

The Top Baby Names in France

Girls	Boys
1. Manon	1. Armand
2. Jade	2. Jules
3. Louise	3. Lucas
4. Alice	4. Léo
5. Camille	5. Gabriel
6. Chloé	6. Arthur
7. Lēa	7. Louis
8. Lou	8. Hugo
9. Emma	9. Tom
10. Charlotte	10. Sacha

The Top Baby names in Spain

Girls	Boys
1. Lucía	1. Hugo
2. María	2. Daniel
3. Paula	3. Pablo
4. Daniela	4. Alejandro
5. Martina	5. Álvaro
6. Carla	6. Adrián
7. Sara	7. David
8. Sofía	8. Mario
9. Valeria	9. Diego
10. Julia	10. Javier

The top baby names in America

Girls	Boys
1. Emma	1. Noah
2. Olivia	2. Liam
3. Sophia	3. Mason
4. Ava	4. Jacob
5. Isabella	5. William
6. Mia	6. Ethan
7. Abigail	7. James
8. Emily	8. Alexander
9. Charlotte	9. Michael
10. Harper	10. Benjamin

The Top Baby Names in Australia

Girls	Boys
1. Olivia	1. Oliver
2. Ava	2. Jack
3. Charlotte	3. James
4. Mia	4. Noah
5. Isla	5. William
6. Sophie	6. Thomas
7. Grace	7. Ethan
8. Amelia	8. Mason
9. Ruby	9. Liam
10. Chloe	10. Lachlan

The Girl Baby Names for 2017 book predicts another year of vintage baby names hitting the top spots. Our top ten predictions are;

Top Ten Baby Name Predictions for 2017	
1. Amelia	1. George
2. Ava	2. Oliver
3. Olivia	3. Jack
4. Isabella	4. William
5. Isla	5. Harry
6. Emily	6. Noah
7. Mia	7. Charlie
8. Jessica	8. Oscar
9. Isabella	9. Lewis
10. Poppy	10. Thomas

Celebrities

New baby name trends often emerge once a popular celebrity has a baby. Both celebrities and pop culture can impact and generate a sudden usage of a baby name, creating a remarkable rise in popularity within such a short period of time. Prominence is often given to a name after a celebrity has chosen it for their own child.

Celebrity culture can have a huge impact on people, influencing parents and helping to inspire them with baby names. Some celebrities like to choose traditional and more vintage baby names for their child, while other celebrities like to turn their backs on tradition and prefer to pick a unique name that can seem outrageous to some. Celebrities can feel pressurised and incentivised to create a unique baby name for their child, the use of objects such as Apple and Pilot are becoming frequently used for baby names along with the use of verbs.

Either way, celebrities can influence parents across the globe on their choice of baby names. The more popular a celebrity, the more influence they are likely to have on the public.

Some of the most talked about celebrity baby names are;

Kim Kardashian and Kanye West

One of the most famous and recent controversial baby names came from the reality TV star Kim Kardashian, and her rapper husband, Kanye West. The celebrity couple named their daughter North West in 2013. The name is said to have been chosen as it represents the highest power. The couple had their second child in December 2015, Saint West.

Lil' Kim and Papers

Lil' Kim and Papers welcomed their baby girl into the world back in June 2014. They named their daughter Royal Reign, which didn't seem so much of a surprise as rapper Lil' Kim likes referring to herself as the 'Queen Bee.'

Liv Tyler and David Gardner

Liv Tyler and her boyfriend choose a nautical baby name for the son Sailor Gene Gardner in early 2015.

Tom Fletcher and Giovanna Fletcher

McBusted star Tom Fletcher and his author wife Giovanna Fletcher named their son Buzz Michelangelo. The married couple insist that the name was not inspired by the famous Toy Story character, Buzz Lightyear. Tom and Giovanna welcomed their second son into the world, Buddy Bob Fletcher in February 2016.

Megan Fox and Brian Austin Green

Hollywood stars Megan Fox and Brian Austin Green raised eyebrows after they named their second son Bodhi Ransom in early 2014. The Buddhism-inspired name Bodhi means awakened or enlightenment on the path to Nirvana. Megan and Brian are expecting their third child in 2016. There has already been much speculation about the possible baby name.

Omarion and Apryl Jones

The R&B singer Omarion and his partner Apryl Jones named their son Megaa Omari Grandberry in 2014. The name is definitely distinctive and one of a kind.

Ciara and Future

Singers Ciara and Future named their son Future Zahir in 2014. Naming your child after its father has been a popular tradition for centuries. However, the name Future was actually taken from his father's stage name.

Holly Madison

Former Playboy model, Holly Madison received quite a lot of criticism after she named her daughter Rainbow Aurora in 2013. Holly defended her baby name choice by claiming that she had always loved the name Rainbow because it is such a pretty and unusual name. She also revealed that the name was inspired by somebody that she went to school with who also had the same name Rainbow. Holly and her husband are currently expecting baby number two due in 2016.

Alicia Silverstone

Hollywood actress Alicia Silverstone named her son Bear Blu back in May 2011. The name is unique and Silverstone claims that most people find the name to be "Super cute."

Nicole Ritchie and Joel Madden

Reality TV star Nicole Ritchie and her musician husband Joel Madden named their son Sparrow James Midnight. Nicole explained that she really liked the name Sparrow which was influenced by Captain Jack Sparrow from The Pirates of the Caribbean. Madden is said to like the name for different reasons. Nicole also revealed that she liked how the name sounded with her daughter's name, Harlow.

Gwen Stefani and Gavin Rossdale

Although musicians Gwen Stefani and Gavin Rossdale have never disclosed the origins of their son's name, Zuma Nesta Rock. There has been much speculation and theories surrounding their baby name choice. Many people believe that Zuma is named after a beach in Malibu where Rossdale is said to have had an epiphany. Nesta is believed to have come from Gwen Stefani's love of reggae music, as it is also the given name of Bob Marley. Finally, Rock is thought to be inspired by the genre of music.

Nicholas Cage

Possibly due to his love of comics, Hollywood actor Nicholas Cage notoriously named his son after the Krypton name of Superman, Kal-El.

Penn Jillette

Renowned magician Penn Jillette believes that it is cruel for parents to give a child a name that others already have, therefore he and his wife decided to call their daughter a very unique and rememberable name, Moxie Crimefighter.

Pop culture names

Movies and successful television shows have had a huge influence on baby names, along with books and music for decades. Names that are given to the leading protagonists typically see an instant increase in the popularity of baby names. The Twilight Saga has popularised the names, Isabella and Jacob, along with other hugely successful names that have been given to vampires in films and television shows such as True Blood and the Vampire Diaries.

Reality television can also have an immense influence on the choice of baby names. Since the Kardashians shot to fame in 2007, there has been a huge rise in baby names beginning with the letter 'K'. The globally successful US television series, Teen Mom has sparked a spectacular surge in the popularity of the baby names Maci and Bentley. Maci Bookout is one of the show's original cast members, and Bentley is the name of her eldest son.

Disney movies inspire people every day with their fairytale stories and beautiful characters. The unique personalities and the inner qualities that the leading characters boast, quite often influence parents-to-be with a list of baby names. In 2010, the girls name Tiana more than doubled with parents giving this name to their daughters after Disney released The Princess and The Frog. Disney princesses have had a huge impact on baby names over the years.

However, it is not only the Disney princesses that inspire parents with new baby names, Disney films have featured a succession of unforgettable heroines and heroes which parents are naming their children after.

Disney Princess Names	
Anna	Frozen
Ariel	The Little Mermaid
Aurora	Sleeping Beauty
Belle	Beauty and The Beast
Elsa	Frozen
Jasmine	Aladdin
Merida	Brave
Moana	Moana
Mulan	Mulan
Pocahontas	Pocahontas
Tiana	The Princess and the Frog
Tinkerbell	Peter Pan

Disney Male Names	
Buzz	Toy Story
Eric	The Little Mermaid
Finn	Cars
Gaston	Beauty and the Beast
Milo	Atlantis
Peter	Peter Pan
Hans	Frozen
Kristoff	Frozen
Remy	Ratatouille
Rex	Toy Story
Sebastian	The Little Mermaid
Woody	Toy Story

Paying homage to a historical figure, classic movie star, musician or celebrity by naming your child after them is a way of demonstrating the admiration and respect that you have for that individual. Hollywood actor Vin Diesel is the latest celebrity to pay homage to a fellow actor by naming his daughter Pauline after the death of his co-star Paul Walker, who tragically died in a car wreck in 2013. Mariah Carey named her daughter Monroe after one of her favourite idols and film stars Marilyn Monroe. Liam Gallagher named his son Lennon after his favourite Beatles star John Lennon.

Different Spellings

Creating new or using different spellings can make your babies name less traditional and also help it to stand out from the crowd. Making up new spellings for a traditional name can also become trendy and quickly generate a new name craze. The name Chloe has seen a modern change in how it is spelled with some parents opting to spell the name with a 'K,' Khloe. Swapping the 'c' with a 'k' has become a popular choice for parents as these letters are easily substitutable with one and other.

Changing or mixing up the vowels, A, E, I, O, U & sometimes Y can create a brand new version of a traditional name. Very occasionally will the vowel from the first letter of a name be changed, it is frequently more common for parents to change the vowels within the name.

Names with Letter C	Names with Letter K
Cameron	Kamron
Carly	Karlee
Cailyn	Kailyn
Caitlyn	Katelyn
Cassandra	Kassandra
Catalina	Katalina
Chloe	Khloe
Danica	Danika
Dominic	Dominik
Eric	Erik
Jacob	Jakob
Lucas	Lukas
Mackenzie	Makenzie
Michaela	Makayla
Marcus	Markus
Nicholas	Nickolas
Zachary	Zakary

Vowel changes	
Aiden	Aidyn
Jayden	Jaiden
Lauren	Lauryn
Reagan	Regan
Zoe	Zoie

One of the most popular ways to modify a name is to add or to remove one or more of the consonants within the name.

Some parents decide to spell their babies name differently from the traditional way as a way to indicate the gender of their child's name. This is particularly common with baby girl names. Adding or removing consonants can create a whole new vibrant name.

There are no set rules on how to spell a name, however being creative with a name's spelling can cause problems in the long run, constantly having to correct people on spellings and pronunciations, which could also cause confusion and embarrassment throughout your child's life.

Adding or removing consonants	
Alana	Alannah
Austin	Austyn
Ava	Avah
Eliana	Elianna
Giselle	Gisselle
Hannah	Hanna
Isabelle	Izabelle
Jackson	Jaxson
Jason	Jayson
Liliana	Lillianna
Madison	Maddison

Destination Names

Destination names may have depth and personal meaning to the parents who choose to give them to their children. The name might tell a personal adventure or a story as well as being exotic and unusual. A destination name could be a destination where the couple first met or dated, where they grew up, or where the child was conceived. It could just be a location loved by the parents from a holiday or somewhere that they have always wanted to visit or live. Destination names can also send out a signal that the parents are worldly travelers.

Alicia Keys and her husband Swizz Beatz named their son Egypt. Alicia said that the name was inspired by a trip and personal journey she went on while visiting Egypt. Her husband suggested that they should use the name for their baby as the holiday was such a life changing and important time for Alicia. The Beckham's famously named their first son Brooklyn after he was apparently conceived there in the late 1990's.

Parents have numerous reasons as to why they chose destination names for their children. Locations can have great significance to people's lives and history. Honoring a city, state, county or a country by giving your baby the same name is a way of telling your story and having it live on through your family tree.

Destination names	
Austin	Lourdes
Boston	Lucia
Bronx	Madison
Brooklyn	Marseille
Carolina	Montana
Catalina	Odessa
Charlotte	Orlando
Chelsea	Oxford
Dakota	Paris
Dallas	Phoenix
Denver	Savannah
Eden (Biblical Garden of Eden)	Shiloh (Biblical city)
Georgie	Sicily
Hamilton	Sonora
Houston	Troy
India	Valencia
Ireland	Venice
Kenya	Vienna
Kingston	Virginia
Lincoln	Zion (Biblical)
London	

Gender neutral names

Gender neutral names are becoming increasingly popular with modern parents. This is most likely due to the fact that there has been a substantial rise with parents who are choosing to raise their child in a gender neutral way with clothes, toys, and unisex baby names. Companies and parents are choosing to break away from the traditions and refusing to reinforce gender stereotypes that have been around for millennia.

Blake Lively and her husband Ryan Reynolds chose the name James Reynolds for their daughter in December 2014. Mila Kunis and Aston Kutcher also chose a gender neutral name for their daughter who they named Wyatt Kutcher in September 2014. Some people believe that a masculine sounding name can be a workplace advantage for the child when it is older.

Is a name truly masculine or feminine? Well, a name will always remain a name; therefore, it is whatever your child is. However, time can make a lot of difference when it comes to gender neutral names. Names that are considered unisex today such as Courtney and Casper may not have even been considered for a girl's name twenty years ago. The more creative the spelling, the more likely that the name is being used for a girl.

Modern names often start off being unisex and then gradually start being spelled differently, thus creating a female version and a male version. Names that end with –on usually imply that the name is being used for a male, whereas names ending with –ynn tend to imply that the name is being used for a female.

Names can shift from being gender neutral to male or female over time. Therefore, if you decide to pick a gender neutral name for your baby, you should be prepared for the name to eventually tilt to being associated with either a male or a female.

When should I announce the baby name?

There is no specific time or rule on when you or your partner should announce your chosen baby name. It is a personal choice, and nobody can tell you when you can and can't do it. You should announce the baby's name when you and your partner feel comfortable and certain with your name choice. I announced my first son's name-to-be when I was seven months pregnant. However, when he was born I didn't go with the name which I had originally chosen for him. This did cause some confusion for family and friends, as I ended up giving my son a completely different name which wasn't even considered during my pregnancy. The name for my second child was chosen during pregnancy by my partner. We both really liked the name and told everybody what the baby would be called. The only thing that we changed between the pregnancy and birth of our son was the spelling of his name. This took a little longer to decide.

Some parents decide to announce their babies name during pregnancy while others prefer to wait until the baby is born. Whether you decide to announce your babies name before or after the birth, you can still have some fun with the announcement. The rise in baby showers has also seen an increase in baby name announcements. You could do this with the use of balloons, cakes or by getting everybody to play a fun guessing game and reveal the baby's name at the very end.

The power of social media has also had a great impact on announcing both pregnancy and baby names. This is because it is an easy and cheap way to make announcements which can also be fun while reaching vast amounts of people who may live all over the world.

Photography is a fun and creative way to announce the baby's name. Some mothers like to take a picture of their pregnant bellies with the chosen baby name stuck onto the belly using a name tag. Others like to place objects on top or in front of the belly that spell out the baby's name. Letter bricks are a popular choice for this method.

If you have more than one child, involving any siblings can be an extremely fun and adorable way to announce the babies name to the world. You could have your child wearing a T-shirt with the baby's name exhibited on the front; they could be holding up a picture with the baby's name spelled out on a chalkboard, easel painting, box, or even on a tablet device. There any many creative ways that you and your family could do this.

Video announcements have seen a rise in baby name announcements.

Parents are opting to use this method to announce their baby's name, the reasons behind their choice and then explaining the meaning of the name. A video announcement could also make a great family keepsake; you could watch the video together in ten or twenty years' time when your child is all grown up and maybe have some children of their own. It's a good way to look back and remember those special family moments.

A new and rising trend with parents are for them to reserve the baby's full name on social media sites, then revealing the name to family and friends with a scan picture of their newborn baby. The pages are then used to update the child's milestones with close friends and family.

Keepsake announcements have a more traditional feeling to them and can be a great keepsake for your family and friends. This can be done by using paper or card announcements with a picture of your baby, weight and size and, of course, the baby's full name.

Decorations and baby nurseries can be a good way to announce the baby's name, with the use of personalised toys, decoration stickers, wall hangers, and door names.

Being creative with food is a fun choice since buying personalised sweets and candy bars has become easier and, therefore, a fun way to make pregnancy and baby name announcements. You could combine this option with the use of photography and social media. Spelling out your baby's name with candy, alphabet spaghetti or other food items, while creating cool and artistic photographs that would make a lovely family keepsake.

The number of parents who are choosing to have a baby naming ceremony to reveal their children's full name has tripled in the past few years. With loved ones gathered together for a non-religious celebration, the name is then presented to family and friends.

Past Trends

Important titles, names which carry a grand sense of importance such as King, Queen, Prince, and Princess have been a highly popular name choice throughout the times. Although these names tended to decline during the 1950's, there has been a recent surge in popularity; this is probably because of the celebrities who are choosing these names for their own children.

'Y' spellings

Replacing a letter in the name with the letter 'y' has been a popular choice since the early twentieth century. During the 1920's it also became highly desirable to add an 'e' to names that already ended with the letter 'y' for example, Bettye, Bobbye and Rubye.

Gems

For centuries valuable gems and precious stones have been a popular choice for baby names. This includes names such as Beryl, Diamond, Opal, Pearl, and Ruby. Other signs of preciousness such as Coral and Goldie have also been a fashionable name choice.

Boy names for girls

Choosing traditional male names and using them as female names became trendy during the late 19th century. The most popular boy's names that were given to girls are Billie, Bobbie, Charlie, Frankie, and Tommie.

Last names for first names

Last names for first names have also been a trendy option for parent's. The names Coleman, Hilton, Preston, Scott, and Spencer are just some of the names that emerged after it became increasingly popular to use surnames as given first names.

A-Z

Baby Girl Names

For 2017

A

Abigail
Pronunciation: AB-ih-gayl
The name Abigail is of Hebrew origin. The meaning of Abigail is "father's rejoicing". A biblical name; borne in the Old Testament by the wife of King David (1 Samuel). Abigail was described as 'good in discretion and beautiful in form'. Abigail referred to herself as David's handmaiden so often that the name became a popular term for a lady's maid. The name was introduced to Britain in the 16th century. Diminutives: Abbey, Abbie, Abby, Abi, Gail, Gale, Gayle.

Ada
Pronunciation: AY-dah
The name Ada is of Old German origin. The meaning of Ada is "noble". The name possibly derives from the Old German Names Eda or Etta. Ada is also used as a short form of the names Adele and Adelaide. The name was borne by a 7th-century abbess of Saint Julien Des Près at Le Mans. The name was introduced to Britain in the 18th century.

Adela
Pronunciation: a-DELL-ah
Adela is of Old German origin. The meaning of the name Adela is "noble". Derived from Old German, athal. The name was introduced to Britain by the Norman invaders. Adela was the name of William the Conqueror's youngest daughter. The name died out during the Middle Ages and was later revived in the 19th century. Diminutives: Addie, Addy, Della.

Adelaide
Pronunciation: AD-a-layd
The name Adelaide is of Old German origin. The meaning of Adelaide is "noble, kind". The name is a Norman French version of the Old German name, Adelheid. The name was borne by the wife of Otto The Great (10th century), Holy Roman Emperor. Queen Adelaide, wife of William IV, popularised the name in the 19th century. The city of Adelaide in Australia is named after her. Diminutives; Addie, Addy.

Adrienne
Pronunciation: AY-dree-en
Adrienne is of Latin origin. The meaning of the name Adrienne is "from Hadria". The name is a French feminine form of Adrian.

Africa
Pronunciation: AF-ree-ca
The name Africa is of Irish Gaelic origin. The meaning of Africa is "pleasant". The name is an Irish Gaelic version of Aifric. Africa is also a place name for the continent.

Agatha
Pronunciation: AG-a-thah
The name Agatha is of Greek origin. The meaning of Agatha is "good". The name is a Latin form of the Greek name, Agathe. Borne by a 3rd-century martyr and saint. She was tortured and murdered at Catania in Sicily after she refused to marry a Roman consul. She is the patron saint of bell ringers. Her feast day is 5th February. The name underwent a popular revival in the 19th century. The name was also made

famous by renowned writer, Agatha Christie (1890-1976).

Agnes

Pronunciation: AG-ness

Agnes is of Greek origin. The meaning of the name Agnes is "chaste, holy". The name is a Latin form of the Greek hagnos. Borne by a young Roman girl who was martyred at the age of thirteen on the orders of Diocletian in c. 304. Agnes had refused several offers of marriage, as she declared herself to be devoted to Christ. She is now regarded as the patron saint of virgins; Her feast day is 21st January. Diminutives: Aggie, Aggy, Ness, Nessa, Nesta.

Ailsa

Pronunciation: a(i)-LIS-ah

Ailsa is of Old Norse origin. The meaning of the name Ailsa is "island of Alfsigr". Ailsa is also a place name, Ailsa Craig in the estuary of the River Clyde. Diminutive: Ailie.

Aimee

Pronunciation: ay-MEE

The name Aimee is of Old French and Latin origin. The meaning of Aimee is "to love, beloved". The name has been used as a first name since the Middle Ages.

Aisha

Pronunciation: ah-EE-shah

Aisha is of Arabic origin. The meaning of the name Aisha is "alive, thriving". Borne by the third wife of Prophet Muhammad. H Rider Haggard popularised the name in his novel, She (1887).

Alannah

Pronunciation: ah-LAH-nah

Alannah is of Irish Gaelic origin. The meaning of the name Alannah is "O my child". From Irish Gaelic, Oleanbh.

Alberta

Pronunciation: al-BER-tah

The name Alberta is of Old English origin. The meaning of Alberta is "noble, bright". The name is a feminine form of the masculine name Albert. Alberta is also the name of the Canadian province, which was named after Princess Louise Alberta.

Alexandra

Pronunciation: al-eks-AHN-dra

The name Alexandra is of Greek origin. The meaning of Alexandra is "man's defender". The name is a feminine form of the masculine name Alexander. The name was popularised in the 19th century when Edward VII married the Danish Princess Alexandra in 1863. Diminutives: Alex, Alexa, Alix, Lex, Lexie, Lexy, Sandie, Sandra, Sandy, Tiggy, Zandra.

Alexis

Pronunciation: a-LEX-iss

Alexis is of Greek origin. The meaning of the name Alexis is "defender". Derived from Greek, Alexios, which means 'to defend'. The name is often used as a shortened variation of the name Alexander. Although Alexis is traditionally a male name, it is now also used for girls in the modern world. Saint Alexis was a popular saint of Edessa, admired as a 'man of God.'

Alice

Pronunciation: AL-iss

The name Alice is of Old German origin. The meaning of Alice is "noble, exalted". Originally a common adaptation of the name Adelaide, Alice became recognized as a first name in its own right. Lewis Carroll popularised the name with his books, Alice's Adventures in Wonderland (1865), and Through the Looking Glass (1872). The main character was based on his childhood friend Alice Lidell.

Amalia

Pronunciation: a-ma-LIA

Amalia is of Latin and Old German origin. The meaning of the name Amalia is "work". The name is a variation of Amelia.

Amanda

Pronunciation: ah-MAN-dah

The name Amanda is of Latin origin. The meaning of Amanda is "loveable". From Latin Amanda, the female form of amare. The name first appeared as a first name on a 1212 birth record from Warwickshire, England. The name was popularised in the 17th century by the playwright and poet, Colley Cibber (1671-1757). Diminutives: Manda, Mandi, Mandie, Mandy.

Amelia

Pronunciation: a-MEEL-yah

Amelia is of Latin and Old German origin. The meaning of the name Amelia is "eager worker, labour". From Old German amal, and influenced by the Latin name Aemelia. Princess Amelia brought the name to Britain in the 18th century. Diminutives: Emily, Millie, Milly.

Amina

Pronunciation: ah-MEEN-ah

The name Amina is of Arabic origin. The meaning of Amina is "honest, peaceful". Amina bint-Wahab was the mother of the Prophet Muhammad.

Amy

Pronunciation: AY-mee

The name Amy is of Old French and Latin origin. The meaning of Amy is "beloved". Amy is an anglicised form of the name Aimèe. Originally used as a nickname for the Latin name Amata. The name was popularised by characters in Louisa M Alcott's Little Women (1868).

Anastasia

Pronunciation: ahn-a-STAH-shah

Anastasia is of Greek origin. The meaning of the name Anastasia is "Resurrection". From the Greek word anastasis, which means 'rising up.' Borne by a Roman saint and matron, she was said to have buried the bodies of Saint Peter and Saint Paul with Saint Basilissa. The name is popular in Eastern Europe in honour of a 4th century Dalmatian martyr. Anastasia was made famous in the 20th century by the daughter of Tzar Nicholas II, the last Russian czar. In

1920, a woman claiming to be Anastasia said that she had survived the massacre of the royal family in 1917, thus generating worldwide publicity.

Andrea

Pronunciation: AN-dree-ah

The name Andrea is of Greek origin. The meaning of Andrea is "manly, virile". The name is a feminine form of the masculine names Andreas and Andrew. The name is also used as a nickname for Alexandra. The name dates back to the 17th century.

Angela

Pronunciation: AN-je-lah

The name Angela is of Greek origin. The meaning of Angela is "angel, messenger of God". The name is a feminine form of Angel and Angelus. The name became popular in Britain from the 18th century. Diminutive: Angie.

Angelica

Pronunciation: an-JEL-ih-kah

Angelica is of Latin origin. The meaning of the name Angelica is "angelic". From the Latin Angelicus. Borne by the heroine of Matteo Boiardo's Orlando Innamorato (1487), Angelica was the beautiful daughter of the king of Cataio. Orlando's passionate love for Angelica ended up driving him mad. Diminutive: Angie.

Angelina, Angeline

Pronunciation: an-JEL-ih-na

The name Angelina is of Italian origin. The meaning of Angelina is "angel, messenger of God". The name Angeline is of French origin. Both Angelina and Angeline are variations of the Greek name Angela. Diminutive: Angie.

Angharad

Pronunciation: an-HAR-ad

The name Angharad is of Welsh origin. The meaning of Angharad is "beloved, much loved". Angharad is a character in the Welsh folk tales Mabinogian.

Anita

Pronunciation: a-NEE-tah

The name Anita is of Spanish origin. The meaning of Anita is unknown. Anita is originally a Spanish diminutive of Ann. The name was made famous by the Swedish film actress, Anita Ekberg.

Ann, Anne

Pronunciation: ANN-e

The name Anne is of English and Latin origin. The meaning of Anne is "God has favoured me". Anne is the English form of the biblical name Hannah.

Anna

Pronunciation: AN-ah

Anna is of Hebrew origin. The meaning of the name Anna is "God has favoured me". Anna is a Latinate variant of the name Hannah. In classical legend, Anna was the sister of Dido, Queen of Carthage. A biblical name; borne in the New Testament by an elderly prophetess (Luke 2:36-38).

Annabel
Pronunciation: AN-a-BELL
The name Annable is of Latin origin. The meaning of Annabel is "loveable". The name is a variation of Amabel. The name has been a popular first name in Scotland since the 12th century.

Anneka
Pronunciation: AN-ee-ka
Anneka is of Swedish origin. The meaning of the name Anneka is "sweet-faced". Anneka is a Swedish form of the name Ann(e).

Anneliese
Pronunciation: AN-ee-lee-se
Anneliese is of German origin. The meaning of the name Anneliese is "Graced with God's bounty". Anneliese is a variant of the Latin name Annalisa. The German name is a compound of Anna and Liese (Elizabeth).

Annette
Pronunciation: an-NET
The name Annette is of French origin. The meaning of Annette is unknown. Annette is a feminine diminutive form of Antoine. Diminutive: Net, Nettie, Netty, Toinette, Toni.

Antoinette
Pronunciation: ann-twa-NET
The name Antoinette is of French origin. The meaning of Antoinette is unknown. Antoinette is a feminine diminutive form of the name Antoine. The name was made famous by the French Queen Marie Antoinette (1755-1793). Diminutives: Net, Nettie, Netty, Toinette, Toni.

Antonia
Pronunciation: ann-TONE-yah
Antonia is of Latin origin. The meaning of the name Antonia is unknown. Antonia is a feminine form of the masculine name Anthony. The name was a common Roman feminine family name. Diminutive: Toni, Tony, Tonia, Tonya.

Anya
Pronunciation: AN-ya
The meaning of Anya is "resurrection; God had favoured me". Anya is a variant of the Greek name Anastasia. The name is an anglicised spelling of the Spanish form of Ann(e).

Aphra
Pronunciation: AFF-rah
The name Aphra is of Hebrew origin. The meaning of Aphra is "young deer". The name is either derived from Hebrew aphrah, which means 'dust' or possibly a variation of the Latin name Afra.

Aoife
Pronunciation: EE-fra
The name Aoife if of Irish, Gaelic, and Scottish origin. The meaning of Aoife is "beautiful". From Irish Gaelic aoibh, which means 'beauty.' The name is borne by numerous heroines in ancient Irish legend. Eva is the anglicised form of the name.

April
Pronunciation: AY-prill
The name April is of Latin origin. The meaning of April is "to open". April is also the name of the fourth month of the year. The name may have been influenced by the French equivalent, Avril.

Arabella
Pronunciation: AIR-a-bell-ah
The name Arabella is of Latin origin. The meaning of Arabella is "prayerful". The name might be a variation of the Annabel. The name has been popular in Scotland since the 14th century and spread to England in the 18th century.

Areta
Pronunciation: A-re-ta
The name Areta is of Greek origin. The meaning of Areta is "virtue, excellence". Areta is related to the name Arethusa. The name is also a variant of the Greek name Aretha.

Ariadne
Pronunciation: ar-ee-AHD-nee
The name Ariadne is of Greek origin. The meaning of Ariadne is "most holy". Borne mythology; Ariadne was the daughter of King Minos of Crete. She helped Theseus to escape by giving him a ball of wool so that he could find his way out of the Labyrinth after he had killed the Minotaur. Saint Ariadne is a 2nd-century saint and Christian martyr.

Arianwen
Pronunciation: a-ree-AN-win
The name Arianwen is of Welsh origin. The meaning of Arianwen is "white, holy silver, fair". Borne in the 5th by a daughter of Brychan, a legendary Welsh chieftain.

Artemis
Pronunciation: AR-te-miss
The name Artemis is of Greek origin. The meaning of Artemis is unknown. Borne in Greek mythology; Artemis was a Greek goddess of the moon, hunting, and of chastity, equivalent to the Roman goddess Diana. Artemis is used as both a boy's name, and as a girl's name.

Astrid
Pronunciation: AS-trid
The name Astrid is of Old Norse origin. The meaning of Astrid is "beautiful goddess". From Old Norse elements áss, which means 'god', and fríor, 'beautiful.'

Athene
Pronunciation: a-THEE-nee
The name Athene is of Greek origin. The meaning of Athene is "immortal". Borne in Greek mythology; Athene was the virgin goddess of arts, wisdom, and war. She was supposedly born fully armed, from the head of Zeus. Athene was a patron of the city of Athens.

Audrey
Pronunciation: AW-dree
The name Audrey is of Old English origin. The meaning of Audrey is "noble strength".

Derived from the informal pronunciation of the name of Saint Etheldreda, 7th-century abbess of Ely.

Aurora

Pronunciation: aw-ROHR-ah
The name Aurora is of Latin origin. The meaning of Aurora is "dawn". Borne in mythology; Aurora was the goddess of sunrise. In various versions of the 'Sleeping Beauty' fairytale, the princess's name is Aurora.

Ava

Pronunciation: AY-vah
The name Ava is of uncertain origin. The meaning of Ava is also unknown. The name is possibly a medieval Germanic diminutive for names that begin with AV-. The name may be a variation of Eva. Hollywood actress Ava Gardner (1922-1990) popularised the name.

Aveline

Pronunciation: AY-v-e-line
Aveline is of Norman origin. The meaning of the name Aveline is unknown. The name is a Latinate form of the Norman French name Eveline.

Avril

Pronunciation: AV-ril
The name Avril is of Latin origin. The meaning of Avril is "to open". From French Avril, which means 'April.' The name may also be a nickname for Averil.

B

Barbara
Pronunciation: BAR-bra
The name Barbara is of Greek and Latin origin. The meaning of Barbra is "strange, foreign woman". The name was originally an onomatopoeic word describing the babbling sound of an unintelligible foreign tongue. The name was applied to anyone who did not speak Greek. Saint Barbara is invoked as a protector against fire and lighting; she is the patron saint of architects, stonemasons, and fortifications. Her father was about to cut off her head when he was struck by lightning. Her actual existence is disputed. Diminutives: Bab, Babs, Barbie, Baubie, Bobby.

Bea
Pronunciation: bea
Bea is a diminutive of the names, Beatrice and Beatrix.

Beatrice, Beatrix
Pronunciation: BEE-a-triss
The name Beatrice is of Latin origin. The meaning of Beatrice is "bringer of joy". The name is mentioned in the Domesday book. Shakespeare used the name in Much Ado About Nothing (1598). The name was revived in the 19th century, possibly after Queen Victoria named one of her daughters Beatrice. Beatrice is also the name of the heroine of Dante's, Divine Comedy (c. 1309-02).

Belinda
Pronunciation: ba-LIN-dah
The name Belinda is of Old German origin. The meaning of Belinda is "snake". From the Old German name Betlindis. Diminutives: Bel, Bell, Belle, Linda, Lundy.

Bella
Pronunciation: BELL-ah
Bella is of Italian and Latin origin. The meaning of the name Bella is "beautiful". The name is also a diminutive of names incorporating the element –bella, such as Isabella.

Bennett
Pronunciation: BEN-et
Bennett is of French and Latin origin. The adopted surname has been used for both girl's and boy's names. Taken from the medieval vernacular form of Benedict.

Bentley
Pronunciation: BENT-lee
The name Bentley is of Old English origin. The meaning of the name Bentley is "bent grass meadow". The adopted surname is used more commonly as a boy's name. However, it is also used as a girl's name. Bentley is also a place name for many places in England.

Bernadette
Pronunciation: ber-na-DET
The name Bernadette is of French and Old German origin. The meaning of Bernadette is "strong, brave bear". Bernadette is a French feminine form of the masculine name Bernard. Saint Bernadette Soubirous popularised the name during the 19th century. She was a French peasant girl who

had visions of the Virgin Mary and uncovered a spring near Lourdes where miraculous cures are sought. Diminutives: Bernie, Berny.

Berta
Pronunciation: BERT-ah
The name Berta is of Old German origin. The meaning of Berta is "bright". The name was borne by the mother of Charlemagne. The name was introduced to Britain by the Normans.

Beryl
Pronunciation: BEHR-el
The name Beryl is of Greek origin. The meaning of Beryl is "light green semi-precious gemstone". From Old French beril, which was derived from Greek berullos, denoting a precious pale green stone with light blue, yellow and white lights. The name was popular during the 19th century.

Beth
Pronunciation: beth
The name Beth is of Hebrew origin. The meaning of Beth is "house". Beth is also a diminutive of the name Elizabeth. The name dates back to the 19th century. Louisa M Alcott popularised the name in her novel, Little Women (1868).

Bethany
Pronunciation: BETH-a-nee
The name Bethany is of Hebrew origin. The meaning of Bethany is "house of figs". A biblical name, Bethany is the name of the village near Jerusalem. Diminutive: Beth.

Bethia
Pronunciation: BE-thia
The name Bethia is of Hebrew origin. The meaning of Bethia is "daughter of God".

Betsy
Pronunciation: BET-see
The name Betsy is of Hebrew origin. The meaning of Betsy is "God is my oath". Betsy is a diminutive of the name Elizabeth.

Bette
Pronunciation: BET-ee
The name Bette is of Hebrew and French origin. The meaning of Bette is "God is my oath". Bette is a French diminutive of the name Elizabeth. The name was popularised by Hollywood actress Bette Davis (1908-1989).

Betty
Pronunciation: BET-ee
The name Betty is of Hebrew origin. The meaning of Betty is "God is my oath". The name was popular during the 20th century.

Beulah
Pronunciation: bea-u-LAH
The name Beulah is of Hebrew origin. The meaning of the name Beulah is "married". A biblical name for the land of Israel (Isaiah 62).

Beverly, Beverley
Pronunciation: BEV-er-lee

The name Beverly is of Old English origin. The meaning of Beverly is "beaver". Beverly is an adopted surname and place name, from Old English beofor. The name was first used as a masculine name in the 19th century. The name is now given to females.

Bianca

Pronunciation: bee-AHNK-ah
The name Bianca is of Italian origin. The meaning of Bianca is "pure, white". The name was used by Shakespeare in The Taming of the Shrew (1593). Bianca was the gentle sister of Katharina, 'the Shrew'. Shakespeare also used the name is Othello (1604).

Billie

Pronunciation: BILL-ee
The name Billie is of Old English origin. The meaning of Billie is unknown. Billie is a diminutive of the names Wilhelmina and William.

Birgit

Pronunciation: ber-GEET
Birgit is of Norwegian origin. The meaning of the name Birgit is "exalted one". Birgit is a variant of the name Bridget. Diminutives: Birgit, Brita, Britt.

Blake

Pronunciation: blayk
Blake is of Old English origin. The meaning of the name Blake is "black", "pale". The adopted surname is used as both a boy's name, and as a girl's name. Blake was originally used as a nickname for someone with skin or hair that was either very dark ("blaec") or very light ("blac").

Blanche

Pronunciation: BLAN-che
The name Blanche is of Old French and Old German origin. The meaning of Blanche is "white, pure". Blanche of Lancaster brought the name to Britain in the 14th century.

Blodwen

Pronunciation: B-lod-wen
The name Blodwen is of Welsh origin. The meaning of Blodwen is "holy flower, white flower". The name was popular in the Middle Ages.

Blossom

Pronunciation: BLOSS-om
Blossom is of Old English origin. The meaning of the name Blossom is "flower-like". The name is a direct adoption of the English vocabulary, denoting a mass of flowers on a fruit tree. Blossom was first used as a first name in the 19th century.

Blythe

Pronunciation: bleeth
The name Blythe is of Old English origin. The meaning of Blythe is "blithe, cheerful". Originally an adopted surname.

Bobbie, Bobby

Pronunciation: BOB-ee
The name Bobbie is of Latin origin. The meaning of Bobbie is "foreign woman".

Bobby is a variant of the Latin name Barbara. The name is also a diminutive of the name Roberta.

Bonita
Pronunciation: boh-NEE-tah
The name Bonita is of Spanish origin. The meaning of Bonita is "pretty". Diminutives: Bonni, Bonny.

Brady
Pronunciation: BRAY-dee
The name Brady is of Irish and Gaelic origin. The meaning of the name is "descendant of Brádach". The name is used as both a boy's name, and as a girl's names.

Branwen
Pronunciation: BRAN-wen
The name Branwen is of Welsh origin. The meaning of Branwen is "raven, fair". Borne in Welsh legend by the heroine of one of the tales of the Mabinogian.

Brenda
Pronunciation: BREN-dah
The name Brenda is of Old Norse origin. The meaning of Brenda is "sword, torch". The name is sometimes considered to be a feminine form of Brendan.

Brennan
Pronunciation: BREN-an
Brennan is of Irish and Gaelic origin. The meaning of the name Brennan is "Teardrop". Brennan is used as both a boy's name, and as a girl's name. The name is also a variant of Brendan.

Bride
Pronunciation: BRI-de
Bride is of Gaelic origin. The meaning of the name Bride is "exalted one". Bride is a variation of the Gaelic name Bridget.

Bridie
Pronunciation: BRID-ee
Bridie is of Gaelic origin. The meaning of the name Bridie is "exalted one". Bridie is a variation of the Gaelic name Bridget.

Bridget
Pronunciation: BRIH-jet
Bridget is of Gaelic origin. The meaning of the name Bridget is "exalted one". Bridget is an anglicized version of the Irish name Brighid. Borne in mythology; Saint Brigid of Kildare (c. 450-525) is the second patron saint of Ireland, after Saint Patrick. Her feast day is 1st February. Diminutives: Biddy, Bridie.

Bridgid
Pronunciation: BRID-gid
The name Bridgid is of Gaelic origin. The meaning of Bridgid is "exalted one". Bridgid is a variation of the name Bridget.

Briony, Bryony
Pronunciation: BRI-on-ee
Briony is of Greek origin. The meaning of the name Briony is "luxurious growth". The name was adopted in the 19th century when botanical names became fashionable.

Brooks
Pronunciation: brux
Brooks is of Old English and Old German origin. The meaning of Brooks is "water", "small stream". Brooks is used as both a boy's name, and as a girl's name.

Bronwen
Pronunciation: BRON-wen
The name Bronwen is of Welsh origin. The meaning of Bronwen is "white breast, blessed breast". Diminutive: Bron.

Bryn
Pronunciation: br-yn
The name Bryn is of Welsh origin. The meaning of the name Bryn is "hill". The name is also a short form of Brynmor. Bryn is used as both a boy's name, and as a girl's name.

C

Caitlín
Pronunciation: KATE-lin
Caitlín is of Old French and Greek origin. The meaning of the name Caitlín is "pure". Caitlín is the Irish Gaelic form of the name Catherine.

Cameron
Pronunciation: KAM-ren
The name Cameron is of Scottish and Gaelic origin. The meaning of Cameron is "crooked nose". Cameron is a Scottish Highlands clan surname. Cameron is used as both a girl's name, and as a boy's name.

Camilla
Pronunciation: ka-MEEL-ah
The name Camilla is of Latin origin. The meaning of Camilla is "helper to the priest". Camilla is a feminine form of the Roman family name Camilus. Fanny Burney popularised the name with her novel, Camilla (1796). Diminutives: Millie, Milly.

Candida
Pronunciation: kan-DEE-dah
The name Candida is of Latin origin. The meaning of Candida is "white". The name is borne by several early saints. Diminutive: Candy.

Carina
Pronunciation: ka-REEN-ah
The name Carina is of Latin origin. The meaning of Carina is "beloved, dear". Carina is a feminine diminutive form deriving from Italian caro.

Carla
Pronunciation: kar-LAH
Carla is of Old German origin. The meaning of the name Carla is "free man". Carla is a feminine form of the masculine name Carl. The name was popular throughout the late 20th century.

Carly
Pronunciation: KAR-lee
The name Carly is of Latin origin. The meaning of Carly is "free man". Carly is a diminutive of the names Carla, Carlotta, and Caroline.

Carmel
Pronunciation: kar-MEL
Carmel is of Hebrew origin. The meaning of the name Carmel is "garden, orchard". A biblical name; Mount Carmel was where Elijah summoned Israel to choose between God and Baal (I King 18). In the 12th century, a monastery was founded dedicated to the Virgin Mary.

Carmela
Pronunciation: kar-MEL-ah
The name Carmela is of Italian origin. The meaning of Carmela is "garden, orchard". Carmela is an Italian variant of the name Carmel.

Carmen
Pronunciation: KAR-men
The name Carmen is of Spanish origin. The meaning of Carmen is "song, charm". The name is originally a Spanish form of the name Carmel, influenced by the Latin word, carmen. The name was popularised

in the 19th century by Bizet's opera, Carmen (1875).

Carol

Pronunciation: KARE-ol

The name Carol is of Old German origin. The meaning of Carol is "free man". Carol is a feminine form of the names Charles, originated from the Latin name Carolus. Originally used as a boy's name, the name is now generally used for girls.

Caroline

Pronunciation: KARE-a-line

The name Caroline is of Old German origin. The meaning of Caroline is "free man". Caroline is a feminine form of the names Charles, originated from the Latin name Carolus. The German-born wife of King George II, Caroline of Ansbach, introduced the name to Britain. Diminutives: Carly, Caro, Carrie.

Carolyn

Pronunciation: KARE-a-lyn

The name Carolyn is of Old German origin. The meaning of Carolyn is "free man". Carolyn is a variant of the name Caroline, dating back to the 20th century.

Carys

Pronunciation: CHAR-is

Carys is of Welsh origin. The meaning of the name Carys is "love".

Casey

Pronunciation: KAY-see

The name Casey is of Irish and Gaelic origin. The meaning of Casey is "alert, watchful". The name Casey is used as both a boy's name, and as a girl's name. Casey is from the Gaelic male name Cathasaigh.

Cassandra

Pronunciation: ka-SAN-dra

Cassandra is of Greek origin. The meaning of Cassandra is "shining upon man". Cassandra is possibly a variation of the name Alexander. The name is borne in Greek mythology by a Trojan princess. She was blessed with the gift of prophecy and foretold the fall of Troy. However, after turning down Apollo's advances, he was so angry that he arranged for her never to be believed. The name was revived in the 18th century. Diminutives: Cas, Cassie, Sandra.

Catherine

Pronunciation: KATH-rin

The name Catherine is of Greek origin. The meaning of Catherine is "pure". Borne by several early saints, Saint Catherine Alexandria was a 4th-century martyr of noble birth. She was condemned to death on a spiked wheel. However, the wheel mysteriously broke. This led to her being beheaded. Saint Catherine Alexandria is the patron saint of wheelwrights. Saint Catherine Siena is (1347-1380) is considered the patron saint of Italy. King Henry VIII had three wives named Catherine. Diminutives: Casey, Cate, Cath, Cathie, Cathy, Kate, Kay, Kit, Kitty.

Cathleen
Pronunciation: kath-LEEN
Cathleen is of Greek origin. The meaning of the name Cathleen is "pure". Cathleen is a variation of the name Catherine and was influenced by the Irish Gaelic name Caitlín.

Catrin
Pronunciation: CAT-rin
The name Catrin is of Greek origin. The meaning of Catrin is "pure". Catrin is a Welsh form of the name Catherine.

Catriona
Pronunciation: cat-REE-ona
Catriona is of Scottish Gaelic and Irish origin. The meaning of the name Catriona is "pure". Catriona is a variation of the name Catherine. Robert Louis Stevenson popularised the name during the 19th century, with his novel Catriona (1893).

Cecilia
Pronunciation: sess-SEEL-yah
The name Cecilia is of Latin and Old Welsh origin. The meaning of Cecilia is "blind, sixth". Cecilia is a Latinate feminine form of the name Cecil. The name was borne in the 2nd century by a blind Roman martyr and saint. She is regarded as the patron saint of musicians and music. Her feast day is 22nd November. The name was popular during the Middle Ages. The name was later revived in the 18th century.
Diminutives: Cis, Ciss, Cissie, Cissy, Sissie, Sissy.

Cecilie
Pronunciation: sess-SEEL-e
The name Cecilie is of Latin and French origin. The meaning of Cecilie is "blind, sixth". Cecilie is a French feminine form of the name Cecil. Cecilie is also a variant of the names Cecilia and Cecily.

Ceinwen
Pronunciation: KAYN-wen
The name Ceinwen is of Welsh origin. The meaning of Ceinwen is "beautiful; gems".

Celeste
Pronunciation: she-LEST
The name Celeste is of Latin origin. The meaning of Celeste is "heavenly". The name was popular among early Christians. Celeste is a masculine form of the name Celestin.

Celine
Pronunciation: SEL-ine
The name Celine is of Latin origin. The meaning of Celine is "heaven". Derived from Latin Caelum, which means 'sky.' The French name is spelled Cèline. The name was popularised by singer Celine Dion.

Ceridwen
Pronunciation: ke-RID-wen
The name Ceridwen is of Welsh origin. The meaning of Ceridwen is "fair, holy, blessed poetry". Borne in Celtic mythology by the Welsh goddess of poetic inspiration.

Chandler
Pronunciation: CHAND-ler

Chandler is of Middle English and Old French origin. The meaning of the name Chandler is "candle maker". The adopted surname was also an occupational name from 'chandele' meaning 'candle'. Chandler is used as both a boy's name, and as a girl's name.

Chandra
Pronunciation: SHAN-drah
Chandra is of Hindi and Sanskrit origin. The meaning of the name Chandra is "moon shining". The greatest Hindu goddess Devi is also known as Chandra.

Chanel
Pronunciation: sha-NELL
Chanel is of Old French origin. The meaning of the name Chanel is "wine, amphora". The name was influenced by the legendary fashion designer Gabrielle 'Coco' Chanel (1883-1971). Chanel is also the name of the 14th-century French missionary saint.

Chantal
Pronunciation: shanh-TAL
Chantal is of Old French origin. The meaning of Chantal is "stone". An adopted surname and place name, after Chantal in Saóne-et-Loire. The name was originally given in honor of Saint Jeanne-Françoise de Chantal (1572-1641). She lived a strict religious life and founded an order of nuns, the Vistandines.

Charlene
Pronunciation: shar-LEEN
The name Charlene is of Old German origin. The meaning of Charlene is "free man". Charlene is a feminine form of the masculine name Charles.

Charlotte
Pronunciation: SHAR-let
The name Charlotte is of Old German origin. The meaning of Charlotte is "free man". Charlotte is a French feminine diminutive of Charles. The name has been used in England since the 17th century. The name was popularised by King George III's wife, Charlotte Sophia (1744-1817). E.B White also popularised the name in Charlotte's Web (1952). Diminutives: Charley, Charlie, Chattie, Chatty, Lottie, Lotty, Totty.

Charmaine
Pronunciation: shar-MAYNE
The name Charmaine is of English origin. The meaning of Charmaine is "charm". A modern coinage derived from the name Carminea. The name was first used by Maxwell Anderson and Laurence Stallings in the play, What Price Glory? (1924).

Chastity
Pronunciation: CHASS-ti-tee
The name Chastity is of Latin origin. The meaning of Chastity is "pure". The virtue name is from Latin castus.

Cherie
Pronunciation: sha-REE

The name Cherie is of French origin. The meaning of Cherie is "darling". From French chère.

Cherry

Pronunciation: CHARE-ee

The name Cherry is of English and Old French origin. The meaning of Cherry is "cherry, tree". Cherry is originally a diminutive of the name Charity. The name later became associated with the sweet fruit. Cherry is also used as a diminutive of Cherie.

Cheryl

Pronunciation: CHER-ell

The name Cheryl is of French and Greek origin. The meaning of Cheryl is "cherry fruit, green gemstone". The name is an early 20th-century variation of the name Cherry.

Chiara

Pronunciation: kee-AH-ra

The name Chiara is of Italian and Latin origin. The meaning of Chiara is "bright, famous". The name is an Italian form of Clara and Claire. The name is borne by several early Italian saints.

Chloe

Pronunciation: KHLOH-ee

Chloe is of Greek origin. The meaning of the name Chloe is "green shoot". The name is associated with the Greek goddess of agriculture and fertility, Demeter. The name was borne in Longus's Greek romance, Daphnis, and Chloe. A biblical name; Chloe is briefly mentioned by Saint Paul in the New Testament (1 Corinthians 1:11). The name was popular with the Puritans during the 17th century.

Christabel

Pronunciation: KRIS-ta-bell

The name Christabel is of Latin and French origin. The meaning of Christabel is "beautiful Christian". The name is a medieval coinage from the name Christ with –bel, from Latin bella. Samuel Taylor Coleridge popularised the name in his poem Christabel (1816). Christabel Pankhurst (1880-1958) was a pioneer suffragette.

Christiana

Pronunciation: kris-TEEN-iah

Christiana is of Latin origin. The meaning of the name Christiana is "follower of Christ". The name is a medieval Latinate form of Christian. John Bunyan used the name for the wife of Christian in The Pilgrims' Progress (1684). Diminutives: Chris, Christie, Christy.

Christina

Pronunciation: kris-TEEN-ah

Christina is of Latin origin. The meaning of the name Christina is "follower of Christ". Christina is a feminine form derived from the Latin name Christianus. Diminutives: Chris, Chrissie, Chrissy, Tina.

Christine

Pronunciation: kris-TEEN

The name Christine is of French and Latin origin. The meaning of Christine is "follower of Christ". Christine is a French form of the name Christina. The name was introduced to Britain in the 19th century. Diminutives: Chris, Chrissie, Chrissy.

Ciara

Pronunciation: kee-AR-ah
The name Ciara is of Irish and Gaelic origin. The meaning of Ciara is "black". Ciara is a modern Irish feminine form of the name Ciaran.

Cindy

Pronunciation: SIN-dee
The name Cindy is of English and Greek origin. The meaning of Cindy is "from Mount Kynthos". Cindy is a diminutive of the name Lucinda. The name became a popular first name in its own right.

Cissy

Pronunciation: sis-EE
The name Cissy is of Latin and Old Welsh origin. The meaning of Cissy is "blind, sixth". Cissy is a diminutive of the names Cecilia and Cicely.

Claire

Pronunciation: clare
The name Claire is of Latin origin. The meaning of Claire is "bright, famous". The Norma invaders introduced the name to Britain in the original form of, Clara. The name was revived in the 19th century as the French form of Clare.

Clara

Pronunciation: KLAR-a
Clara is of Latin origin. The meaning of the name Clara is "bright, famous". Clara is a feminine form of the Latin adjective clarus. The name has largely been replaced by the names Chiara, Claire, and Clare.

Clare

Pronunciation: clare
The name Clare is of Latin origin. The meaning of Clare is "bright, famous". The name was a popular medieval English form of the name Clara.

Clarissa

Pronunciation: kla-RISS-ah
Clarissa is of Latin origin. The meaning of the name Clarissa is "most bright, most famous". Clarissa is a Latinate form of the name Clarice. Samuel Richardson popularised the name in his novel Clarissa (1748).

Claudia

Pronunciation: KLAW-dee-ah
The name of Claudia is of Latin origin. The meaning of Claudia is "lame". Claudia is a feminine form derived from the Roman family name Claudius. A biblical name; borne by a Christian woman of Rome greeted by Paul in his second letter to Timothy (2 Timothy 4). The name dates back to the 16th century.

Claudine

Pronunciation: klaw-DEEN

The name Claudine is of French origin. The meaning of Claudine is "lame". Claudine is a French feminine and diminutive form of the name Claude. The name was popular throughout the 20th century.

Cleo
Pronunciation: KLEE-oh
Cleo is of Greek origin. The meaning of the name Cleo is "glory of the father". Cleo is a diminutive of the Greek name Cleopatra. The name became a popular first name in its own right.

Clíodhna
Pronunciation: KOR-ee
The name Clíodhna is of Irish Gaelic origin. The meaning of Clíodhna is unknown. The name is born in Irish legend; Clíodhna was one of the three beautiful daughters of the poet Libra.

Coco
Pronunciation: KO-ko
Coco is of French origin. The meaning of the name Coco is "people of victory". Coco is a diminutive of Nicolette, and also of names starting with CO-. The name was popularised by the famous fashion designer Gabrielle Coco Chanel (1883-1971).

Cody
Pronunciation: KO-dee
The name Cody is of Irish and Gaelic origin. The meaning of the name Cody is "Helper". Cody is used as both a boy's name, and as a girl's name.

Cole
Pronunciation: kohl
Cole is of Middle English and Old French origin. The meaning of Cole is "charcoal". Originally a surname that was derived from a medieval given name. Cole is used as both a boy's name, and as a girl's name.

Colette
Pronunciation: ko-LET
The name Colette is of French and Greek origin. The meaning of Colette is "people of victory". Colette is a diminutive of the name Nicolette. The name is borne by a 15th-century French nun and saint; she was renowned for giving her money to the poor. French writer, Sidonie-Gabrielle Colette (1873-1954) popularised the name.

Colleen
Pronunciation: kah-LEEN
The name Colleen is of Gaelic origin. The meaning of Colleen is "girl, wench". Colleen is an Irish vernacular word, which means girl. The name is also used as a feminine form of the masculine name Colin.

Concetta
Pronunciation: CON-cetta
The name Concetta is of Italian and Latin origin. The meaning of Concetta is "conceived, conception". Concetta is an Italian form of a Latin name, concepta. The name is a reference to the Immaculate Conception.

Constance
Pronunciation: KAHN-stans
The name Constance is of Latin origin. The meaning of Constance is "constant, steadfast". From the Latin Constantia, which means 'constancy.' The name was introduced to Britain by the Normans. The name was borne by a virgin saint daughter of Constantine the Great. Diminutive: Connie.

Constantia
Pronunciation: CONST-ant-tia
The name Constantia is of Latin origin. The meaning of Constantia is "constant, steadfast". Constantia is Latin form of Constance. The name was popular with early Christians and also with the Puritans. Diminutive: Connie.

Corey
Pronunciation: KOR-ee
The name Corey is an English surname derived from an Old Norse personal name Kori. Corey is used as both a boy's name, and as a girl's name. The meaning of the name may mean "God, peace."

Corinna, Corinne
Pronunciation: ko-RINN-nah
The name Corinna is of Greek origin. The meaning of Corinna is "maiden". Corinna was an alternative name for Persephone, and also for a 5th-century poetess. Roman poet Ovid used the name for the woman in his love poetry. The name was later revived in the 16th and 17th centuries.

Cosima
Pronunciation: KOZ-i-ma
The name Cosima is of Greek origin. The meaning of Cosima is "beauty, order". Cosima is a feminine form of Cosmo.

Courtney
Pronunciation: COURT-ney
Courtney is of Old French origin. The meaning of Courtney is "domain of Curtis". The name is both a surname and a place name. Courtney is a Norman baronial name from places in Northern France called Courtenay. Courtney is used as both a boy's name, and a girl's name.

Crystal
Pronunciation: KRISS-tal
The name Crystal is of Greek origin. The meaning of Crystal is "ice". Derived from Greek krustallos. Crystal is one of the several stone and mineral names that became fashionable in the late 19th century.

D

Dabney
Pronunciation: DAB-nee
The name Dabney is of Old French origin. The meaning of Dabney is "from Aubigny".

Dacey
Pronunciation: DAY-cee
The name Dacey is of Irish and Gaelic origin. The meaning of Dacey is "from the South".

Dacia
Pronunciation: DAY-sha
Dacia is of Latin origin. The meaning of the name Dacia is unknown. Originally a place name, Dacia was a Roman province.

Dada
Pronunciation: DA-da
The name Dada is of Nigerian origin. The meaning of Dada is "curly haired".

Dagmar
Pronunciation: DAG-mar
The name Dagmar is of Old German and Scandinavian origin. The meaning of Dagmar is "glorious, day's glory". Dagmar is a royal name in Denmark.

Dagny
Pronunciation: DAG-ny
The name Dagny is of Old Norse origin. The meaning of Dagny is "new day". The name possibly relates to the Old German name Dagmar.

Dahlia
Pronunciation: DAL-yah
Dahlia is of Swedish and Scandinavian origin. The meaning of the name Dahlia is "Valley".

Daisy
Pronunciation: DAY-zee
The name Daisy is of Old English origin. The meaning of Daisy is "day's eye". The name was first used as a diminutive of the French name, Marguerite. Daisy is a reference to the flower of the same name that opens during the day. The name was popular during the 19th century when botanical names became fashionable. Henry James also popularised the name in his novel Daisy Miller (1878).

Damaris
Pronunciation: DAM-a-ris
The name Damaris is of Greek and Latin origin. The meaning of Damaris is "calf, to tame". A biblical name; borne by an Athenian woman who heard Paul speak at Mar's Hill, she was converted by Saint Paul (Acts 17). The name was adopted by the Puritans.

Dana
Pronunciation: DAY-nah
The name Dana is of Old English origin. The meaning of Dana is "from Denmark". Borne in mythology; Dana was the Celtic goddess of fertility. The name is also used a Scandinavian feminine form of Daniel.

Daniella
Pronunciation: dan-YELL-ah
The name Daniella is of Hebrew and French origin. The meaning of Daniella is

"God is my Judge". Daniella is a feminine form of the masculine name Daniel. Daniella is the Latinate form. Diminutives: Dan, Dani.

Danielle
Pronunciation: dan-YELL
The name Danielle is of Hebrew and French origin. The meaning of Danielle is "God is my Judge". Danielle is a feminine form of the masculine name Daniel. The name has been used as a first name since the 20th century. Daniella is the Latinate form. Diminutives: Dan, Dani.

Daphne
Pronunciation: DAFF-nee
The name Daphne is of Greek origin. The meaning of Daphne is "laurel tree". Borne in Greek mythology; by the daughter of the river god Peneus in Thessaly. Daphne had vowed to die a virgin as she fled Apollo's advances. The gods felt sorry for Daphne and turned her into a laurel tree. The name was popular in the 18th and 20th centuries.

Dara
Pronunciation: DAR-ah
The name Dara is of Hebrew origin. The meaning of Dara is "charity, nugget of wisdom".

Darcy
Pronunciation: DAR-cee
The name Darcy is of Irish and Gaelic origin. The meaning of Darcy is "dark". An adopted Norman baronial surname (D'Arcy). The name was introduced to Britain during the Norman Conquest. Darcy is used as both a boy's name, and as a girl's name. Darcy is also a Norman place name.

Daria
Pronunciation: DAR-ee-ah
The name Daria is of Greek and Persian origin. The meaning of Daria is "maintains possessions well". Daria is a feminine form of the masculine name Darius.

Darrell
Pronunciation: DA-rr-ELL
The name Darrell is of French and English origin. The meaning of Darrell is unknown. Originally an adopted surname, derived from a French place name, Arielle (French region of Calvados). The name is used as both a girl's name, and as a boy's name.

Davina
Pronunciation: dah-VEE-nah
Davina is of Hebrew and Scottish origin. The meaning of the name Davina is "beloved". Davina is a Scottish feminine form of the name David. The name dates back to the 17th century. Diminutives: Vina, Vinia.

Dawn
Pronunciation: dorn
Dawn is of Old English origin. The meaning of the name Dawn is "the first appearance of light". The name is a direct vocabulary adoption. The name dates back to the 20th century.

Deborah
Pronunciation: DEB-er-ah
The name Deborah is of Hebrew origin. The meaning of Deborah is "Bee". A biblical name; borne by two figures in the Old Testament. One is a prophetess and judge who summoned Barak to battle against an invading army (Judges 4), the other is the nurse of Rebekah (Genesis 35). The name was adopted by the Puritans. Diminutives: Deb, Debbie, Debby, Debs.

Dee
Pronunciation: dee
The name Dee is of Welsh origin. The meaning of Dee is "swarthy". Dee is a diminutive of any name beginning with the letter 'D'.

Delia
Pronunciation: DEEL-yah
The name Delia is of Greek origin. The meaning of Delia is "visible, from Delos". The name derives from Delos, which is the smallest of the Greek islands of the Cyclades. Delia is also used as a diminutive of names ending in –delia.

Delilah
Pronunciation: dee-LYE-lah
Delilah is of Hebrew origin. The meaning of the name Delilah is "amorous, seductive". A biblical name; borne in the Old Testament by the mistress of Samson, she famously persuaded Samson into revealing the secret of his superhuman strength. She then betrayed him by cutting off his hair as he slept (Judges 16). The name was adopted by the Puritans.

Della
Pronunciation: DEL-ah
The name Della is of German origin. The meaning of Della is "noble". Della is a diminutive of Adela. The name has been a popular first name since the late 19th century.

Delora
Pronunciation: del-OR-ah
The name Delora is of Latin origin. The meaning of Delora is "from the seashore".

Delphine
Pronunciation: DEL-fee-ne
The name Delphine is of French origin. The meaning of Delphine is "woman of Delphia, dolphin". Derived from the Latin name Delphina. The name is the French form of a name which refers to the Greek town of Delphia, home of Apollo's oracle. The Greeks believed that Delphi was the earth's womb.

Denise
Pronunciation: de-NEES
Denise is of French origin. The meaning of the name Denise is "follower of Dionysius". Denise is a French feminine form of the name Denis. The name was first used in Britain in the 12th century.

Dervla
Pronunciation: DER-vlah

The name Dervla is of Irish and Gaelic origin. The meaning of Dervla is "poet's daughter". From the Irish Gaelic name Deirbhile. The name has undergone a revival in Ireland.

Desdemona

Pronunciation: des-de-mona

The name Desdemona is of Greek origin. The meaning of Desdemona "wretchedness". Desdemona is the Latinate form of Greek dysaimon, which means, 'ill-starred, miserable.' Shakespeare used the name in Othello (1604). Desdemona was the beautiful wife of Othello, wrongly accused of adultery which led to her murder.

Devon

Pronunciation: DEV-en

Devon is of English origin. The meaning of the name Devon is uncertain. Devon is originally an adopted surname, English county name, and the name of several towns in America. The name is used as both a boy's name, and as a girl's name.

Diana

Pronunciation: dy-ANN-ah

The name Diana is of Latin origin. The meaning of the Diana is "divine". Borne in mythology; Diana was an ancient Roman goddess of fertility, hunting, and the moon. Her name was possibly derived from Latin divinus. The name has been used as a first name since the 16th century. The name was made famous by the Princess of Wales, Diana (1961-1997).

Diane

Pronunciation: DIA-ane

The name Diane is of French and Latin origin. The meaning of Diane is "divine". Diane is the French form of Diana, the name dates back to the Renaissance.

Dillan

Pronunciation: DILL-an

The name Dillan is of Irish and Gaelic origin. The meaning of Dillan is "like a lion, loyal". The name is a variant of Dillon. Dillan is used as both a boy's name, and as a girl's name.

Dinah

Pronunciation: DYE-nah

Dinah is of Hebrew origin. The meaning of the name Dinah is "judgement". A biblical name: borne by the daughter of Jacob and Leah.

Dolores

Pronunciation: dor-LOR-iss

The name Dolores is of Spanish origin. The meaning of Dolores is "Maria of the sorrows". From Spanish, 'Maria de los Dolores', which is a reference to the Virgin Mary. Diminutives: Lola, Lolita.

Dominica, Domenica

Pronunciation: dom-ih-NEEk-ah

The name Dominica is of French and Latin origin. The meaning of Dominica is "Lord". Dominica is a feminine form of the masculine name Dominic.

Dominque

Pronunciation: dom-ih-NEEK

The name Dominque is of French and Latin origin. The meaning of Dominque is "Lord". Dominque is the French form of the masculine name Dominic.

Donna

Pronunciation: DON-nah

Donna is of Italian origin. The meaning of the name Donna is "woman". The name was an American coinage of the 1920's.

Dora

Pronunciation: DOR-ah

The name Dora is of Greek origin. The meaning of Dora is "gift". Dora is a diminutive of the names Pandora, Dorothea, Dorothy, and Theodora. The name became a popular first name in its own right.

Dorothea

Pronunciation: DOR-o-thee-ah

The name Dorothea is of Greek origin. The meaning of Dorothea is "gift of God". Saint Dorothea was a virgin martyr; she was killed under Diocletian in c. 300. Diminutives: Dora, Thea.

Dulcie

Pronunciation: DUL-cie

The name Dulcie is of Latin origin. The meaning of Dulcis is "sweet". From Latin dulcis. The name was revived in the 19th century.

E

Eartha
Pronunciation: ER-thah
The name Eartha is of Old English origin. The meaning of Eartha is "earth". From Old English eorthe. The name was used by the Puritans in the 17th century.

Edina
Pronunciation: ED-ina
The name Edina is of Old English origin. The meaning of Edina is unknown. The name may be a variation of Edwina, or of Aithne.

Effie
Pronunciation: EFF-ee
Effie is of Greek origin. The meaning of the name Effie is "well spoken". Effie is a diminutive of Euphemia. The name is also used as a nickname for Efrata and Evelyn.

Eileen
Pronunciation: eye-LEEN
The name Eileen is of Irish origin. The meaning of Eileen is unknown. Eileen is an anglicised form of the Irish name Eibhlin. Diminutive: Eily.

Eithne
Pronunciation: EE-na
The name Eithne is of Irish and Gaelic origin. The meaning of Eithne is either, "little fire" or "kernel". The name is borne by several figures in Irish legend.

Elaine
Pronunciation: ee-LAYNE
The name Elaine is of Greek origin. The meaning of Elaine is "sun ray". Elaine is a French form of the name Helen. In Arthurian legend, the name was borne by a character who fell in love with Lancelot. The name underwent a popular revival in the late 19th century.

Eleanor
Pronunciation: EL-a-nor
Eleanor is of Old French and Old German origin. The meaning of the name Eleanor is "sun ray, other". Eleanor is a French form of the name Helen. The name was brought to Britain in the 12th century by Henry II wife, Eleanor of Aquitaine. Diminutives: Ellie, Nell, Nellie, Nelly.

Elena
Pronunciation: eh-LAYN-ah
Elena is of Greek origin. The meaning of the name Elena is "sun ray". Elena is a variation of the name Helen. The name dates back to the 12th century. The name is considered to be an Italian and Spanish form of Helen.

Elise
Pronunciation: el-LEES
Elise is of French and Hebrew origin. The meaning or the name Elise is "God is my oath". Elise is a French diminutive of Elizabeth. The name became popular in its own right, particularly during the 19th century.

Elizabeth
Pronunciation: ee-LIZ-a-beth
The name Elizabeth is of Hebrew origin. The meaning of Elizabeth is "God is my oath". A biblical name; borne in the Old

Testament by the wife of Aaron. In the New Testament the Greek form, Elisabeth was borne by the wife of Zacharias, and mother of John the Baptist. The Greek form of Elisabeth was replaced in the 16th century by Elizabeth, probably due to the reign of Queen Elizabeth I of England. Diminutives: Bess, Bessie, Bessy, Beth, Eliza, Libby, Lisbeth, Liz, Liza, Lizbeth, Lizzie, Lizzy, Tetty.

Ella

Pronunciation: EL-ah
The name Ella is of Old German origin. The meaning of Ella is "all". The name is derived from the Old German name Alia. The name was introduced to Britain by the Normans. The name was later revived in the 19th century.

Ellen

Pronunciation: EL-en
The name Ellen is of Greek origin. The meaning of Ellen is "sun ray". Ellen is the most common variant of the name Helen. The name is also used as a diminutive of Eleanor. The name was first used as an independent name in the 16th century. Diminutives: Ellie, Nell, Nellie, Nelly.

Eloise

Pronunciation: el-o-WEE
The name Eloise is of Old German origin. The meaning of Eloise is "famous warrior". Eloise is the French variant of the name Louise.

Elsa

Pronunciation: EL-sah
The name Elsa is of Hebrew origin. The meaning of Elsa is "God is my oath". Elsa is originally a German diminutive of the name Elisabeth. The name became a popular first name in its own right.

Emanuela

Pronunciation: e-man-u-elah
The name Emanuela is of Hebrew origin. The meaning of Emanuela is "God is with us". Emanuela is a feminine form of the masculine name Emanuel.

Emily

Pronunciation: EM-i-lee
Emily is of Latin origin. The meaning of the name Emily is "rival, eager". Emily is a feminine form of the Roman family name Aemilius. Boccaccio, a 14th-century writer, popularised the name with the form, Emilia. Chaucer used the name in the form Emelye in The Knight's Tale. The name was extremely popular during the 18th 19th and 20th centuries. Diminutives: Millie, Milly.

Emma

Pronunciation: EM-ah
The name Emma is of Old German and Old French origin. The meaning of Emma is "entire, universal". The name was introduced to Britain in the 11th century by Emma of Normandy. The name was a royal name in medieval England. The name was revived in the 18th century, possibly due to Jane Austen's romance novel, Emma

(1815). Emma has been one of the most favoured names for girls in Britain since the 1970's.

Emmeline

Pronunciation: EM-a-leen

The name Emmeline is of Old French and Old German origin. The meaning of Emmeline is "entire, work". Emmeline is the Old French form of the Old German name Ameline. The name was introduced to Britain by the Normans. The name was made famous by Emmeline Pankhurst, a British political activist, and leader of the British suffragette movement. The Suffragette's helped women to win the right to vote.

Erica

Pronunciation: AIR-a-ka

The name Erica is of Old Norse origin. The meaning of Erica is "complete ruler". Erica is a feminine form of the masculine name Eric. Erica is also the name of a species of plants, which includes heather and rhododendrons. The name was revived during the 19th century when botanical names became fashionable.

Erin

Pronunciation: AIR-en

Erin is of Gaelic and Irish origin. The meaning of the name Erin is "Ireland". Derived from the Irish Gaelic name Éirinn. Erin is an ancient poetic name for Ireland.

Esmè, Esmèe

Pronunciation: EZ-may

The name Esmè is of Old French origin. The meaning of Esmè is "esteemed". From Latin aestimatus. The name was introduced to Scotland from France in the 16th century. The name was originally used for both sexes; it is now mainly given to females.

Esmeralda

Pronunciation: ez-mer-AHL-dah

The name Esmeralda is of Spanish origin. The meaning of Esmeralda is "Emerald". Victor Hugo popularised the name with his heroine in the classic, The Hunchback of Notre Dame (1831). Esmeralda was a gypsy girl loved by Quasimodo.

Estella, Estelle

Pronunciation: EST-el-lah

The name Estella is of Old French origin. The meaning of Estella is "star". Charles Dickens popularised the name within his epic novel, Great Expectations (1861). Estelle is the modern French form.

Esther

Pronunciation: ESS-tar

The name Esther is of Persian origin. The meaning of Esther is "star, myrtle". A biblical name; borne in the Old Testament by a young beautiful Hebrew woman. She became the wife of the Persian king Ahasuerus in the 5th century BC after he had rejected his disobedient wife, Vashti. Her story is told in the Old Testament book and in the Apocrypha's Rest of Esther. The name has traditionally been given to girls born during the period of Purim. The name was popular with the Puritans in the 17th century.

Étain
Pronunciation: E-tain
The name Étain is of Irish Gaelic origin. The meaning of Étain is unknown; it could mean "jealousy". Étain is a traditional Irish Gaelic name. Borne in Irish legend by a fairy princess whose wooing by the mortal King Eochaidh, was turned into an opera, The Immortal Hour (1914).

Ethelinda
Pronunciation: e-thelin-da
The name Ethelinda is of Old English origin. The meaning of Ethelinda is "noble serpent". The name was revived in the 19th century.

Etta
Pronunciation: ETT-ah
The name Etta is of English origin. The meaning of Etta is "happy".

Eva
Pronunciation: AY-vah
The name Eva is of Hebrew origin. The meaning of Eva is "alive". Eva is a Latinate form. Harriet Stowe popularised the name with her novel, Uncle Tom's Cabin (1852). Eva (Evangeline) was the name of her heroine. Diminutives: Evie, Evita.

Eve
Pronunciation: eve
Eve is of Latin and Hebrew origin. The meaning of the name Eve is "alive". A biblical name; borne in the Old Testament by the first woman on earth. Eve is described as, 'the mother of all living'. Diminutives; Eveleen, Evie.

Evelyn
Pronunciation: EV-e-lyn
Evelyn is of Norman origin. Anglicised form of the Norman French feminine name Aveline. Evelyn is used as both a boy's name, and as a girl's name. The name was adopted as a boy's name in the 17th century. Originally a surname and used as a given name.

F

Fabia

Pronunciation: fah-BIA

The name Fabia is of Latin origin. The meaning of Fabia is "bean". A Latin feminine form of the Roman family name Fabius.

Fabiana

Pronunciation: fah-BE-ann-ah

The name Fabiana is of Latin origin. The meaning of Fabiana is "bean". A Latin feminine form of the Roman family name Fabius.

Fabiola

Pronunciation: fah-bee-OH-lah

The name Fabiola is of Latin origin. The meaning of Fabiola is "bean". A Latin feminine form of the Roman family name Fabius. Fabiola is a feminine diminutive of the masculine name Fabian. Saint Fabiola was a 4th-century member of the Fabius family, who founded the first hospital for sick and needy pilgrims. Queen Fabiola of Belgium was a Spanish princess.

Fadia

Pronunciation: FAD-ee-a

The name Fadia is of Arabic origin. The meaning of Fadia is "savior". Fadia is a feminine form of Fadi.

Fadila

Pronunciation: FAD-il-ah

The name Fadila is of Arabic origin. The meaning of Fadila is "moral excellence". Fadila is a feminine form of Fadile.

Faida

Pronunciation: FAI-da

The name Faida is of Arabic origin. The meaning of Faida is "plentiful".

Faith

Pronunciation: faith

The name Faith is of Middle English origin. The meaning of Faith is "belief". Faith is one of the three great Christian virtues, with hope and charity. The name is also one of the several abstract nouns denoting admirable personal qualities. The name was used throughout the 16th century and was popular among the Puritans.

Fallon

Pronunciation: FAL-en

The name Fallon is of Irish and Gaelic origin. The meaning of Fallon is "superiority, leader". An adopted surname, anglicised from the Irish surname O Fallamhain, meaning 'leader.' Originally an occupational surname for a textile worker. The name was popularised by the American television series Dynasty.

Fanny

Pronunciation: FAN-ee

The name Fanny is of Latin origin. The meaning of Fanny is "from France". Fanny is diminutive of Frances. The name was extremely popular in the 18th and 19th centuries.

Farah

Pronunciation: FAH-rah

Farah is of Arabic origin. The meaning of the name Farah is "pleasant, joy".

Farrah
Pronunciation: FAH-rah
The name Farrah is a modern coinage of the Arabic name Farah, which means "pleasant, joy." The name was popularised by American actress Farrah Fawcett.

Fatima
Pronunciation: FAH-tee-mah
The name Fatima is of Arabic origin. The meaning of Fatima is "baby's nurse, abstainer". Borne by the Prophet Muhammad's favourite daughter, wife of Haidar, she was the only daughter to bear children.

Fay
Pronunciation: fay
The name Fay is of uncertain origin. The meaning of Fay is "belief, fairy". The name is possibly a diminutive of Faith.

Faye
Pronunciation: faye
The name Faye is of uncertain origin. The meaning of Faye is "belief, fairy". The name is possibly a diminutive of Faith.

Felicity
Pronunciation: fa-LISS-a-tee
The name Felicity is from Old French and Latin origin. The meaning of Felicity is "good fortune, lucky". The name is derived from Latin Felicitas. The name was a virtue name and one of the several abstract nouns denoting admirable personal qualities. The name was first used in the 17th century and was popular with the Puritans.

Fern
Pronunciation: fern
The name Fern is of Old English origin. The meaning of Fern is "fern". From Old English fearn, denoting a green shade-loving plant. Fern is also used as a nickname for Fernanda.

Ffion
Pronunciation: FEE-on
The name Ffion is of Welsh origin. The meaning of Ffion is "white, fair". The name is a Welsh form of Fiona.

Fifi
Pronunciation: FEE-fee
The name Fifi is of French origin. The meaning of Fifi is "Jehovah increases". Fifi is a French variant of the name Josephine. The name is also used as a diminutive for Fiona.

Fina
Pronunciation: FI-na
The name Fina is of Spanish origin. The meaning of Fina is "Jehovah increases". Borne in the 13th century by a woman of San Gimignano, in Tuscany. Fina was a young girl whose claim to be recognised as a saint lay in the perfect resignation with which she accepted bodily suffering. Fina was not martyred. Instead she died of a physical disease. For six years, she lay on a plank in one position, unable to turn or move. Her feast day is 12 March.

Finella
Pronunciation: fin(el)-la
The name Finella is of Gaelic origin. The meaning of Finella is "white, fair". Finella is an Anglicised Scottish form of the Gaelic name Fionnuala.

Finola
Pronunciation: f(i)-no-la
The name Finola is of Gaelic origin. The meaning of Finola is "white, fair". Finola is an Anglicised form of the Gaelic name Fionnuala.

Fiona
Pronunciation: fee-OWN-ah
The name Fiona is of Scottish and Gaelic origin. The meaning of Fiona is "white, fair". Fiona is a Latin form of Gaelic fionn. The name was first used by James Macpherson (1736-1796) in his Ossianic poems. William Sharp later used the name, Fiona Macleod, as a pen-name for his romantic novels.

Fionnuala
Pronunciation: fya-NOO-lah
The name Fionnuala is of Irish Gaelic origin. The meaning of Fionnuala is "white, fair". Borne in Irish legend; Fionnuala was the daughter of King Lir. Who was transformed into a swan and condemned to wander over the lakes and rivers until Christianity came to Ireland.

Flavia
Pronunciation: FLAH-vee-ah
The name Flavia is of Latin origin. The meaning of Flavia is "yellow hair". Flavia is a feminine form of the Roman family name, Flavius. The name was also borne by several early saints.

Fleur
Pronunciation: F-leur
The name Fleur is of Old French origin. The meaning of Fleur is "Flower".

Flick
Pronunciation: F-li-CK
The name Flick is of Latin origin. The meaning of Flick is "lucky". Flick is also a byname from Felicity.

Flo
Pronunciation: flo
The name Flo is of Latin origin. The meaning of Flo is "flowering, in bloom". Flo is a diminutive of the names Flora and Florence.

Flora
Pronunciation: FLO-ra
The name Flora is of Latin origin. The meaning of Flora is "Flower". From the Roman family name Florus, derived from flos. Borne by the Roman goddess of spring and flowers. Her festivals, the Floralia were held on the 28th April- 3rd May. Flora is also the name of a ninth-century Spanish martyr saint. Diminutives: Flo, Florrie.

Florence
Pronunciation: FLOR-ens

Then name Florence is of Latin origin. The meaning of Florence is "flowering, in bloom". Florence is a medieval form of the Latin name Florentius. Florence Nightingale (1820-1910) popularised the name during the 19th century. She was named after the Italian city where she was born. The name was later revived in the 20th century. Diminutives: Flo, Florrie, Foss, Flossie, Floy.

Florrie
Pronunciation: FLOR-ee
The name Florrie is of Latin origin. The meaning of Florrie is "flowering, in bloom". Florrie is a diminutive of the name Florence.

Floss
Pronunciation: flo-ss
The name Floss is of Latin origin. The meaning of Floss is "flowering, in bloom". Floss is a diminutive of the name Florence.

Fortune
Pronunciation: for-TUNE
Fortune is of Latin origin. The meaning of the name Fortune is "good fate". Borne in mythology; Roman goddess of fortune, chance, and happiness. The name was adopted in the 17th century by Puritans.

Frances
Pronunciation: FRAN-siss
Frances is of Latin origin. The meaning of the name Frances is "French". Frances is a feminine form of Francis. Diminutives: Fanny, Fran, Francie, Frankie, Frannie.

Francesca
Pronunciation: fran-CHESS-kah
Francesca is of Italian and Latin origin. The meaning of the name Francesca is "French". Francesca is an Italian feminine form of Francisco. Borne in the 13th century by Francesca di Rimini, the daughter of Guido da Polenta, Count of Ravenna. Francesca married Giovanni Malatesta. However, she loved his brother Paolo. When Francesca and Paolo were discovered together, they were put to death in c.1289. Her love story has been retold in literature; Dante told the story in his Inferno v. Numerous tragic plays have been written on the subject.

Francine
Pronunciation: fran-SEEN
The name Francine is of French and Latin origin. The meaning of Francine is "French". The name is a familiar form of Françoise, which is the French form of Frances.

Francoise
Pronunciation: fran-co-see
The name Francoise is of Spanish and Latin origin. The meaning of Francoise is "French". Francoise is a Spanish form of the name Frances.

Frederica
Pronunciation: fred-er-EE-kah
The name Frederica is of Old German origin. The meaning of Frederica is

"peaceful ruler". Frederica is a Latinate feminine form of the name Frederick.

Freya
Pronunciation: FRAY-ah
Freya is of Old Norse origin. The meaning of the name Freya is "lady, mistress". Borne in Scandinavian mythology; Freya is the goddess of love, marriage and the dead. The fifth day of the week, Friday was named after her.

Frieda
Pronunciation: FREE-dah
The name Frieda is of German origin. The meaning of Frieda is "Lady, peace". Frieda is a diminutive of numerous names that derive from the Old German element frid.

Fulgencia
Pronunciation: FUL-gen-cia
The name Fulgencia is of Latin origin. The meaning of Fulgencia is "giving off light".

Fulvia
Pronunciation: FUL-via
The name Fulvia is of Latin origin. The meaning of Fulvia is "dusky".

Fruma
Pronunciation: FRU-ma
The name Fruma is of Yiddish origin. The meaning of Fruma is "deeply religious".

G

Gabriela

Pronunciation: GAB-re-el-AH

Gabriela is of Hebrew origin. The meaning of the name Gabriela is "heroine of God". Gabriela is a feminine form of the name Gabriel. Gabriela is the Latinate form. Gabriella is the Italian form. Diminutives: Gaby, Gabby.

Gabrielle

Pronunciation: gab-ree-ELL

The name Gabrielle is of Hebrew origin. The meaning of Gabrielle is "heroine of God". Gabrielle is a feminine form of the name Gabriel. Gabrielle is the French form. Diminutives: Gaby, Gabby.

Gada

Pronunciation: ga-DAH

The name Gada is of Hebrew origin. The meaning of Gada is "fortunate".

Gaea

Pronunciation: GAY-ah

Gaea is of Greek origin. The meaning of the name Gaea is "the earth". Born in mythology; the womanly personification of the earth and mother of the Titans.

Gaetana

Pronunciation: gae-tan-AH

The name Gaetana is of Italian and Latin origin. The meaning of Gaetana is "from Gaeta". Gaeta is a region in southern Italy.

Gaia

Pronunciation: gab-GA-iah

The name Gaia is of Greek origin. The meaning of Gaia is "the earth". Borne in Greek mythology; the goddess of the earth, she gave birth to the sky, mountains, and sea.

Gail

Pronunciation: gayl

The name Gail is of Hebrew origin. The meaning of Gail is "father of exaltation". Gail is a diminutive of the name Abigail. The name became a popular first name in its own right. The name came to Britain in the 20th century.

Galina

Pronunciation: ga-LEEN-ah

Galina is of Greek origin. The meaning of the name Galina is "calm". Derived from the Greek name Galen.

Gaynor

Pronunciation: gay-NOR

The name Gaynor is of Welsh origin. The meaning of Gaynor is "white, soft". Gaynor is a medieval English form of the name Guinevere.

Gavrila

Pronunciation: gav-ril-AH

The name Gavrila is of Hebrew origin. The meaning of Gavrila is "heroine of God".

Gemma

Pronunciation: JEM-ah

Gemma is of Latin origin. The meaning of the name Gemma is "jewel, gem". Derived from the Old Italian word for 'jewel'. The name is borne by Saint, Gemma Galgani (1878-1903). She is known as 'The Daughter of Passion.'

Geneva
Pronunciation: JEN-eve-ah
The name Geneva is of Old French origin. The meaning of Geneva is "juniper tree". The name may refer to the Swiss city, or possibly be a variation of the name Jennifer.

Geneviève
Pronunciation: JEN-a-veev
The name Geneviève is of French origin. The meaning of Geneviève is "white wave". Saint Geneviève (c. 422-512) is the patron saint of Paris. She is said to have defended Paris against the depredations of Attila the Hun with prayer. Her feast day is 3rd January.

Georgette
Pronunciation: jorj-ETT
The name Georgette is of French and Italian origin. The meaning of Georgette is "farmer". Georgette is a French feminine form of the masculine name George.

Georgia
Pronunciation: JOR-jah
Georgia is of Greek and Latin origin. The meaning of the name Georgia is "farmer". Georgia is a feminine form of the masculine name George. The name was influenced by the name of the US state, which was named after King George II of England.

Georgina
Pronunciation: jor-JEE-nah
Georgina is of Latin origin. The meaning of the name Georgina is "farmer". Georgina is a feminine form of the name George. The name was popular during the 18th and 19th centuries.

Georgie
Pronunciation: jorj-EE
Georgie is of Greek and Latin origin. The meaning of Georgie is "farmer". Georgie is a diminutive of Georgette, Georgia, Georgiana or Georgina. Georgia is a feminine form of the masculine name George.

Geraldine
Pronunciation: jare-ul-DEEN
The name Geraldine is of Old German and French origin. The meaning of Geraldine is "spear ruler". Geraldine is a feminine form of the name Gerald. The name was coined in the 16th century by Henry Howard, Earl of Surrey. He used the name in his poems to Lady Elizabeth Fitzgerald, 'the Fair Geraldine'. Diminutives: Geri, Gerry.

Geri
Pronunciation: JER-ee
The name Geri is of English origin. The name is a modern variation of the name Gerry. British singer Geri Halliwell popularised the name during the 1990's.

Germaine
Pronunciation: jer-MAYNE
The name Germaine is of Latin and French origin. The meaning of Germaine is "brother, German". Germaine is a feminine form of the French name Germain. Borne

by a 16th-century French saint, Germaine Cousin (1579-1601).

Gerry

Pronunciation: JER-ee

The name Jerry is of uncertain origin. The meaning of Gerry is "spear ruler". Gerry is a diminutive of the name Geraldine.

Gigi

Pronunciation: JEE-jee

Gigi is of French origin. The meaning of the name Gigi is "bright promise". Gigi is a diminutive of the name Gilberte. The name was popularised by Colette's novel Gigi (1944).

Gilda

Pronunciation: JILL-dah

The name Gilda is of Old English origin. The meaning of Gilda is "golden, gilded". The name was popularised in the 1940's with the Hollywood film, starring Rita Hayworth Gilda (1946). The film starred Rita Hayworth.

Gill

Pronunciation: GILL

The name Gill is of uncertain origin. The meaning of Gill is "bright promise, youthful". Gill is a diminutive of the masculine name Gilbert. The name was popular during the Middle Ages.

Gillian

Pronunciation: GILL-ee-an

The name Gillian is of Latin origin. The meaning of Gillian is "youthful". Gillian is a feminine form of the name Julian. The name was popular during the Middle Ages. Diminutives: Gill Gillie, Gilly.

Gina

Pronunciation: GEE-nah

The name Gina is of uncertain origin. Gina is diminutive of girls' names that end in – gina, such as Georgina. The name became a popular first name in its own right.

Ginger

Pronunciation: JIN-jer

The name Ginger is of English origin. The meaning of Ginger is "liveliness, ginger". Ginger is a diminutive of the name Virginia. Ginger is also the name of a pungent root used as a spice. The name was popularised in the 20th century by the Hollywood dancer, Ginger Rogers (1911-1995).

Gisela

Pronunciation: gi-sel-LAH

The name Gisela is of Old German origin. The meaning of Gisela is "pledge, hostage". From Old German, gisil.

Gita

Pronunciation: gi-TAH

The name Gita is of Hindi and Sanskrit origin. The meaning of Gita is "song".

Glenn

Pronunciation: gl-ENN

The name Glenn is of Scottish Gaelic origin. The meaning of the name Glenn is "Glen, Valley". Originally an adopted surname. The name is used as both a boy's name, and as a girl's name.

Glory

Pronunciation: glo-EE

Glory is of Latin origin. The meaning of the name Glory is "glory". The name is an anglicised form of the Latin name Gloria.

Glyn

Pronunciation: glin

The name Glyn is of Irish and Gaelic origin. The meaning of Glyn is "valley of water". Glyn is a place name. The name is also a variant of Glen. Glyn is used as both a boy's name, and as girl's name

Goldie

Pronunciation: GOLD-ee

Goldie is of English origin. Goldie is a modern by name for one who has blonde hair. Hollywood actress Goldie Hawn popularised the name.

Grace

Pronunciation: grayce

Grace is of Latin origin. The meaning of the name Grace is "blessing, heavenly favour". The name is one of the several abstract nouns denoting admirable personal qualities that became popular first names among the Puritans during the 16th century. The name was revived in the 19th century. Diminutives: Gracie.

Gráinne

Pronunciation: gron-YAH

The name Gráinne is of Irish Gaelic origin. The meaning of Gráinne is "love". Borne in Irish legend; Gráinne was the daughter of King Cormac.

Greta

Pronunciation: GREH-tah

The name Greta is of German origin. The meaning of Greta is "pearl". Greta is a German diminutive of the name Margareta. Hollywood actress, Greta Garbo (1905-1992) popularised the name during the 20th century.

Gretchen

Pronunciation: GREH-chen

Gretchen is of German origin. The meaning of the name Gretchen is "pearl". Gretchen is a German diminutive of the name Margaret. The name became a popular first name in its own right.

Guinevere

Pronunciation: GWIN-a-veer

The name Guinevere is of Welsh origin. The meaning of Guinevere is "fair and smooth". Borne in Arthurian legend by Arthur's unfaithful wife, Queen Guinevere.

Gulielma

Pronunciation: guile-l-MAH

The name Gulielma is of Italian and Old German origin. The meaning of Gulielma is "will helmet". Gulielma is a feminine form of Wilhelm.

Gunhilda

Pronunciation: gun-HIL-dah

The name Gunhilda is of Old Norse origin. The meaning of Gunhilda is "Battle maid".

Gustava
Pronunciation: gust-av-AH
The name Gustava is of Swedish origin. The meaning of Gustava is "staff of the gods". Gustava is a feminine form of the name Gustave, a royal name in Sweden.

Gwen
Pronunciation: gwyn
Gwen is of Welsh origin. The meaning of the name Gwen is "fair, holy, white". Gwen was originally a diminutive of the name Gwendolyn. The name became a popular first name in its own right. The name was popular during the 19th and 20th centuries.

Gwenda
Pronunciation: gwyn-DAH
Gwenda is of Welsh origin. The meaning of the name Gwenda is "fair, good".

Gweyneth
Pronunciation: gwyn-ETH
The name Gweyneth is of Welsh origin. The meaning of Gweyneth is "blessed, happy". The name was popular during the 19th and 20th centuries. Diminutive: Gwyn.

Gwyn
Pronunciation: GW-in
The name Gwyn is of Welsh origin. The meaning of Gwyn is "fair, blessed, holy, white". The name is used as both a boy's name, and as a girl's name.

Gypsy
Pronunciation: GYP-see
The name Gypsy is of Old English origin. The meaning of Gypsy is "Gypsy". The tribe of Romany was called 'gypsy,' as they were thought to have originated in Egypt.

H

Hannah

Pronunciation: HAN-ah

Hannah is of Hebrew origin. The meaning of the name Hannah is "God has favoured me". A biblical name; borne by the mother of the prophet Samuel (I Samuel 1). Unable to conceive, she asked God to bless her with a child, and her prayer was answered. Therefore, the name connotes, 'God has graced me with a son'. The name was adopted by the Puritans in the 17th century. Hannah was a popular girls' name in the 20th century.

Harriet

Pronunciation: HARE-ee-et

The name Harriet is of Old German origin. The meaning of Harriet is "home leader". The name is an anglicised form of Henriette. Harriet is also a feminine form of the masculine name Henry. Diminutives: Hal, Hattie, Hatty, Hettie, Hetty.

Hayley

Pronunciation: HAY-ley

The name Hayley is of Old English origin. The meaning of Hayley is "hay meadow". The name is an adopted surname, originally from a place name. The name became popular in the 20th century when Mary Hayley Bell and Sir John Mills named their daughter Hayley Mills in 1946. Hayley Mills went on to become a famous Hollywood actress.

Hazel

Pronunciation: HAY-zel

The name Hazel is of Old English origin. The meaning of Hazel is "the hazel tree". The name was introduced as a first name during the 19th century when Hazel enjoyed a popular surge as a first name as plant names became fashionable. The name also refers to a specific eye colour.

Heather

Pronunciation: HEH-ther

The name Heather is of Middle English Origin. The meaning of Heather is unknown. From Old English hadre, which donates as a species of moorland shrub with purple and white flowers that, thrives on peaty barren lands. Heather is one of the most popular of the flower names that became fashionable during the 19th century.

Hebe

Pronunciation: HE-be

The name Hebe is of Greek origin. The meaning of Hebe is "youthful beauty". Borne in Greek mythology; Hebe was a daughter of Zeus and Hera, she was the goddess of youth and cup-bearer to the gods. The name was adopted in the 19th century for a species of plant that is native to New Zealand.

Heidi

Pronunciation: HYE-dee

Heidi is of Old German origin. The meaning of the name Heidi is "exalted nature". The name is a Swiss diminutive of Adelheid, from the Old German name Adelaide. Johanna Spyri popularised the name with her beloved children's novel, Heidi (1881). Heidi was the name given to the orphaned heroine.

Helen

Pronunciation: HEL-en

Helen is of Greek origin. The meaning of the name Helen is "sun ray". The name is an Anglicised form of the Greek name Helene. In classical legend, Paris abducted Zeus's mortal daughter, Helen of Troy, an act that resulted in the Trojan War. Helen was, 'the face that launched a thousand ships'. Diminutives: Ena, Hels, Lena, Nell, Nellie, Nelly.

Helena

Pronunciation: HEL-en-a

Helena is of Latin origin. The meaning of Helena is unknown. The name is a Latinate form of Helen. Saint Helena (c. 248-328) was the mother of Constantine the Great. Her purity allowed her to find the True Cross at Jerusalem. Her feast day is 18th August.

Heloise

Pronunciation: HEL-oh-ees

The name Heloise is of French and Old German origin. The meaning of Heloise is "famous warrior". The name was popularised by the true story of the French philosopher Peter Abelard (1079-1142), and his seventeen-year-old student and lover, Hèloíse. After Abelard's castration, he entered the monastery of Saint Denis. Hèloíse later became a nun.

Henrietta, Henriette

Pronunciation: HEN-ree-ett

The name Henriette is of Old German origin. The meaning of Henriette is "home leader". Henriette is a feminine form of Henry. Henriette is a French form of Henry that was introduced to Britain in the 17th century, after Charles I married the French Princess Henriette-Marie in 1625. Diminutives: Etta, Ettie, Etty, Hen, Hennie.

Hermione

Pronunciation: her-MY-oh-nee

The name Hermione is of Greek origin. The meaning of Hermione is "daughter of Hermes, messenger". The name is a feminine form of Hermes, the Greek messenger of God. Borne in mythology; Hermione was the daughter of Helen and Menelaus. Shakespeare also used the name in A Winter's Tale (1611).

Hero

Pronunciation: HE-ro

The name Hero is of Greek origin. The meaning of Hero is unknown. Borne in Greek legend by a priestess of Venus and beloved by Leander. He swam to her nightly across the Hellespont until one night when he accidently drowned. Hero then drowned herself in the same sea as Leander following his death. Shakespeare also used the name Hero in Much Ado About Nothing (1598).

Hilary

Pronunciation: HILL-a-ree

The name Hilary is of Latin origin. The meaning of Hilary is "cheerful". Medieval form of the Latin name Hilarius. Borne by a

4th-century saint and a 5th-century pope. The name was given to both girls and boys name, although it is increasingly rare for boys.

Holly
Pronunciation: HAH-lee
Holly is of Old English origin. The meaning of the name Holly is "the holy tree". From Old English holen, which denotes a species of evergreen plant with prickly leaves. Holly was one of the numerous flower and plant names that became popular first names during the 19th century. The name is often given to girls who are born at Christmas time. Audrey Hepburn popularised the name when Capote's novel, Breakfast at Tiffany's (1958) was turned into a film in 1961. Hepburn played the fascinating heroine, Holly Golightly.

Honor
Pronunciation: AHN-er
The name Honor is of Latin origin. The meaning of Honor is "woman of honor". Honor was one of the several abstract nouns denoting admirable personal qualities that became popular among Puritans in the 16th century. The name was used as both a girl's name, and as a boy's name.

Honey
Pronunciation: HUN-ee
Honey is of Old English origin. The meaning of the name Honey is "nectar". The name is often used as a nickname for endearment.

Hope
Pronunciation: HO-pe
Hope is of Old English origin. The meaning of the name Hope is "belief". One of the three great Christian virtues (faith, hope, & charity). The name is one of the several abstract nouns that symbolizes admirable personal qualities. The name was popular among the Puritans in the 16th century.

I

Ianthe
Pronunciation: eye-AH-thee
The name Ianthe is of Greek origin. The meaning of Ianthe is "violet flower". Borne in Ovid's Metamorphoses, written in the 1st century, Ianthe was a Cretan girl who married Iphis.

Ida
Pronunciation: EYE-dah
Ida is of Greek and Old German origin. The meaning of the name Ida is "hardworking". From Old German id, which means 'work.' The name was introduced to Britain by the Norman's. Borne in Greek mythology; a Greek nymph who cared for the infant Zeus on Mount Ida.

Idris
Pronunciation: E-dris
The name Idris is of Arabic and Welsh origin. The meaning of Idris is "fiery leader, Prophet". Borne in Welsh legend by a giant magician, astronomer, and prince whose observatory was on Cader Idris. Described in the Koran, the Arabic name was borne by a man described as 'a true man' and 'a prophet', he was also the founder of the first Shiite dynasty (788-974). The name is used as both a boy's name and as a girl's name.

Ilsa
Pronunciation: I-lsa
Ilsa is of German origin. The meaning of the name Ilsa is "God is my oath". Ilsa is a diminutive of the Hebrew name Elisabeth.

Iman
Pronunciation: ee-MAHN
The name Iman is of Arabic origin. The meaning of Iman is "belief, faith".

Imogen
Pronunciation: I-mo-gen
The name Imogen is of Irish and Gaelic origin. The meaning of Imogen is "maiden". From the Celtic name Innogen. The name was first used by Shakespeare in his play, Cymbeline (1609). Imogen was the name of the heroine.

India
Pronunciation: IN-dee-ah
The name India is of English origin. Originally the name of the country. India was first used as a name in Margaret Mitchell's epic novel Gone With The Wind (1936).

Ingrid
Pronunciation: ING-rid
The name Ingrid is of Old Norse origin. The meaning of Ingrid is "fair". Borne in Norse mythology; Ing was the God of earth's fertility. The name was popularised by the Hollywood actress Ingrid Bergman (1915-1982).

Iola
Pronunciation: eye-OH-lah
The name Iola is of Greek origin. The meaning of Iola is "violet colored dawn".

Iolana
Pronunciation: eye-oh-LAH-nah

Iolana is of Hawaiian origin. The meaning of the name Iolana is "to soar like the hawk".

Iolanthe
Pronunciation: eye-oh-LAHN-thee
The name Iolanthe is of Greek origin. The meaning of Iolanthe is "violet flower".

Ione
Pronunciation: eye-OHN
The name Ione is of Greek origin. The meaning of Ione is "violet". Ione is also a flower name. The name may have become popular as a first name during the 19th century when botanical names became fashionable.

Irene
Pronunciation: eye-REEN
The name Irene is of Greek origin. The meaning of Irene is "peace". Borne in Greek mythology; Irene was a goddess of peace and wealth. Saint Irene (4th century) was one of the three sisters martyred for their faith in Macedonia.

Iris
Pronunciation: EYE-riss
Iris is of Greek origin. The meaning of the name Iris is "Rainbow". Borne in Greek mythology; Iris was a goddess of the rainbow and messenger of the gods. She rode on rainbows that formed as a bridge, linking heaven and the earth so that she could deliver messages from Olympus. The name was revived in the 19th century. Iris is also a flower name.

Irma
Pronunciation: IR-ma
The name Irma is of Old German origin. The meaning of Irma is "entire, universal".

Isabel
Pronunciation: iz-a-bel
Isabel is of Hebrew origin. The meaning of the name Isabel is "God is my oath". Isabel is a Spanish variant of the name Elizabeth. The name was brought to Britain from France in the form of Isabella by Edward II (1296-1358) French wife. The name was popular throughout Britain until the end of the 17th century. Diminutives; Bel, Bell, Bella, Belle, Ib, Ibbie, Ibby, Isa, Iz, Izzie, Izzy, Tibby.

Isabella
Pronunciation: IZ-a-bel-LA
Isabella is of Hebrew origin. The meaning of the name Isabella is "God is my oath". Isabella is a Latinate form of Isabelle. The name has been a popular throughout Britain since the 18th century.

Isadora
Pronunciation: IZ-a-DOR-ah
The name Isadora is of Greek and Latin origin. The meaning of Isadora is "gift of Isis". The name is a feminine form of Isidore. Acclaimed American dancer, Isadora Duncan (1887-1927) popularised the name.

Isla
Pronunciation: EYE-la

The name Isla is of uncertain origins. Isla is the name of a Scottish river.

Isra

Pronunciation: eyes-ra

The name Isra is of Arabic origin. The meaning of Isra is "night journey". The name is a reference to Muhammad's journey to Jerusalem, in which he met Moses and Jesus.

Itzel

Pronunciation: it-zel

The name Itzel is of Spanish origin. The meaning of Itzel is "star of the aurora sky". Itzel is also the name of a Mayan princess.

Ivana

Pronunciation: ee-VAH-nah

Ivana is of Hebrew and Slavic origin. The meaning of the name Ivana is "God is gracious". Ivana is a feminine form of the masculine names Ivan and John.

Ivette

Pronunciation: ee-VET

The name Ivette is of French origin. The meaning of Ivette is unknown. The name is a variant of Yvette.

Ivonne

Pronunciation: ee-VON

Ivonne is of French origin. The meaning of the name Ivonne is unknown. Ivonne is variant of the name Yvonne.

Ivory

Pronunciation: EYE-vree

Ivory is of Latin origin. The meaning of the name Ivory is "creamy white colour". Ivory is the name used for the hard tusk on animals, which is also used for carving fine art and jewelry.

Ivy

Pronunciation: EYE-vee

The name Ivy is of Old English origin. Ivy is a name from nature, an evergreen climbing plant which represents fidelity and eternity.

J

Jacinta
Pronunciation: JAC-in-ta
The name Jacinta is of Spanish origin. The meaning of Jacinta is "hyacinth". Jacinta is Spanish for of the Greek name Hyacinth. The name was originally used for both sexes. However, today it is mostly used as a girl's name.

Jacqueline, Jacquelyn
Pronunciation: JAK-ah-lin
The name Jacqueline is of French and Hebrew origin. The meaning of Jacqueline is "he who supplants". Jacqueline is a feminine form of Jacques. The name was introduced to Britain in the 13th century. Diminutives: Jackie, Jacky, Jacqui.

Jade
Pronunciation: JAY-de
The name Jade is of English origin. The meaning of Jade is "precious stone". Jade is also a jewel name, of a green stone which was believed to have magical powers of providing protection against disorders of the intestines. The name was derived from archaic Spanish piedra de ijada, which means, 'stone of the side.'

Jamie
Pronunciation: JAY-mee
The name Jamie is of Hebrew origin. The meaning of Jamie is "he who supplants". Jamie is a diminutive of the masculine name James. The name became a popular first name in its own right. Jamie is used as both a girl's name and as a boy's name.

Jancis
Pronunciation: JAN-cis
The name Jancis is a modern blend of Jan and Frances. The name was probably first used by Mary Webb in her novel Precious Bane (1924).

Jane, Jayne
Pronunciation: jayn
The name Jane is of Hebrew origin. The meaning of Jane is "God is gracious". Jane is a feminine form of the masculine name John, derived from the Old French name Jehane. Henry VIII's (d 1537) third wife, Jane Seymour popularised the name during the 16th century. The name was extremely popular in the 18th and 19th centuries. Charlotte Brontë contributed to the popularity of the name with her renowned novel, Jane Eyre (1847).

Janet
Pronunciation: JAN-et
The name Janet is of Scottish origin. The meaning of Janet is unknown. Janet is a feminine form of the masculine name John, originally a medieval diminutive of Jane. The name was popular throughout Scotland and underwent a revival in the 20th century. Diminutives: Jan, Jennie, Jenny.

Janice
Pronunciation: JAN-iss
The name Janice is originally a diminutive of the name Jane. The name was influenced by names that end in –ice, such as Candice and Bernice. The name became popular in its own right during the early 20th century.

Jasmine
Pronunciation: JAZ-min
Jasmine if of Old French and Persian origin. The meaning of the name Jasmine is "Jasmine". From Arabic Jasamine, donating a species of an ornamental climbing plant, which has delicate yellow and white flowers. Disney popularised the name with the film Aladdin (1990). Princess Jasmine was the name of the heroine.

Jean
Pronunciation: jeen
Jean is of Hebrew origin. The meaning of the name Jean is "God is gracious". Jean is a feminine form of the masculine name John. The name was popular throughout Britain during the 20th century. Diminutives: Jeanie, Jeannette, Jeannie.

Jena
Pronunciation: JEN-ah
Jena is of Arabic and Sanskrit origin. The meaning of Jena is "little bird, endurance".

Jeanette
Pronunciation: je-NET
The name Jeanette is of Hebrew origin. The meaning of Jeanette is "God is gracious". Jeanette is a diminutive of the Hebrew name Jean. The name became a popular first name in its own right.

Jeanne
Pronunciation: je(an)-ne
The name Jeanne is of French and Hebrew origin. The meaning of Jeanne is "God is gracious". Jeanne is a feminine form of the masculine name John. Diminutives: Jeannette, Jeannine.

Jemima
Pronunciation: je-MYE-mah
Jemima is of Hebrew origin. The meaning of the name Jemima is "dove". A biblical name; borne in the Old Testament by the eldest of Job's daughters. The name was adopted by the Puritans. Beatrix Potter popularised the name with her heroine, Jemima Puddleduck.

Jennifer
Pronunciation: JEN-ee-fer
The name Jennifer is of English origin. The meaning of Jennifer is "fair and smooth". Jennifer is a variant of Guinevere. The name was popular throughout Britain during the 20th century.

Jessica
Pronunciation: JESS-a-kah
The name Jessica is of Hebrew origin. The meaning of Jessica is "He sees". The name may be a Shakespearean invention for the daughter of Shylock in The Merchant of Venice (1596). Diminutives: Jess, Jessie.

Jessie
Pronunciation: JESS-ee
The name Jessie is of Hebrew origin. The meaning of Jessie is "He sees". Jessie is a Scottish diminutive of the name Janet. The

name dates back to the 18th century. Jessie is also a diminutive of the name Jessica.

Jillian

Pronunciation: JIL-ee-an
The name Jillian is of unknown origin. Jillian is a modern variation of the name Gillian. Diminutives: Jill, Jilly.

Jinny

Pronunciation: JIN-ee
Jinny is of uncertain origin. The name is a variation of Jenny or a diminutive of the name Virginia.

Joan

Pronunciation: jone
The name Joan is of Hebrew origin. The meaning of Joan is "God is gracious". Joan is a feminine form of the masculine name John. Borne by the only female pope, supposedly of the 13th century. However, her existence is still in dispute. The name was replaced by Jane by the 17th century. Hollywood actress Joan Crawford popularised the name during the 20th century.

Joanna

Pronunciation: joh-AN-ah
Joanna is of Latin origin. The meaning of Joanna is "God is gracious". Joanna is a feminine form of the masculine name John. Derived from the Latin name Johanna. A biblical name; borne by several women who were disciples of Christ. The Puritans adopted the name. The name was later revived in the 18th century. Diminutive: Jo, Joey.

Joanne

Pronunciation: JOH-anne
The name Joanne is of uncertain origin. From the Old French name Johanne, derived from the Latin name Johanna. The name was first used as a first name in French-speaking communities in the US. The name became popular during the 20th century. Diminutives: Jo, Joey.

Jocasta

Pronunciation: JO-cast-ah
The name Jocasta is of Greek origin. The meaning of Jocasta is "shining moon". Borne in Greek mythology; Jocasta was a daughter of Meneceus and Queen consort of Thebes, Greece. She was also the wife of Laius, mother of Oedipus, and both mother and grandmother of Antigone, Eteocles, Polynices and Ismene. She unknowingly became the wife of her own son, when the truth was revealed she hung herself.

Jocelin, Joceline

Pronunciation: JOS-e-lin
The name Jocelin is of Old German origin. The meaning of Jocelin is "one of the Goths". The name was introduced to Britain by the Normans. Jocelin is used as both a boy's name, and as a girl's name. Diminutives: Joss, Jossy.

Jocelyn

Pronunciation: JOS-e-lyn

The name Jocelyn is of Old German origin. The meaning of Jocelyn is "one of the Goths". The name was introduced to Britain by the Normans. Jocelyn is used as both a boy's name, and as a girl's name. Diminutives: Joss, Jossy.

Johanna

Pronunciation: joh-HAHN-ah
Johanna is of Latin and Hebrew origin. The meaning of the name Johanna is "God is gracious". The name is originally a Latinate and feminine form derived from Johannes (John).

Jordan

Pronunciation: JOR-dan
Jordan is of Hebrew origin. The meaning of the name Jordan is "down-flowing". From the name of the river in the Middle East where Christ was baptized by John the Baptist. The name has been used as a first name since the Crusades. The name underwent a popular revival in the 1980's. Jordan is used as both a boy's name, and as a girl's name.

Josephine

Pronunciation: JOH-sa-feen
The name Josephine is of Hebrew origin. The meaning of Josephine is "Jehovah increases". Josephine is a feminine form of the masculine name Joseph. Napoleon Bonaparte's wife, Empress Josèphine (1763-1814) popularised the name across Europe. Diminutives: Fifi, Jo, Joey, Josa, Josette, Josie, Josy, Posie, Posy.

Joy

Pronunciation: joy
The name Joy is of Old French origin. The meaning of Joy is "joy". The name is a direct adoption of the English vocabulary. The name was used during the Middle Ages and was popular with the Puritans. The name was later revived in the 19 century.

Judith

Pronunciation: JOO-dith
The name Judith is of Hebrew origin. The meaning of Judith is "Jewess, from Judea". A biblical name; borne in the Old Testament by a wife of Esau. Judith was a central figure in the Apocrypha's Book of Judith. The name was popular during the 18th and 20th centuries. Diminutives: Jodi, Jodie, Jody, Jude, Judi, Judy.

Judy

Pronunciation: JOO-dee
The name Judy is of Hebrew origin. The meaning of Judy is "Jewess, from Judea". Judy is a diminutive of the name Judith.

Julia

Pronunciation: joo-lee-AH
The name Julia is of Latin origin. The meaning of Julia is "Jove's child" Julia is a feminine form of the Roman family name Julius. Shakespeare used the name in The Two Gentlemen of Verona (1594). The name was extremely popular in Britain during the 18th century. Diminutives: Jules.

Juliana

Pronunciation: joo-lee-AH-NAH

The name Juliana is of Latin origin. The meaning of Juliana is "youthful, Jove's child". Juliana is a feminine form of Julian; the name dates back to the Middle Ages.

Julianne
Pronunciation: joo-lee-AH-ne
The name Julianne is a 20th-century coinage of uncertain origin. Julianne is a combination of the names Anne and Julie.

Julie
Pronunciation: JOO-lee
The name Julie is of French origin. The meaning of Julie is "youthful, Jove's child". Julie is a French form of the Latin name Julia. The name was first used in Britain in the 20th century. Julie became one of the most popular girl's names during the 1070's.

Julienne
Pronunciation: JOO-lee-ene
The name Julienne is of French origin. The meaning of Julienne is "youthful, Jove's child". Julienne is a French feminine form of the masculine name Julian.

Juliet
Pronunciation: joo-lee-ET
The name Juliet is of Latin origin. The meaning of Juliet is "youthful, Jove's child". Juliet is a diminutive of the name Julia. Shakespeare popularised the name with the infamous love story, Romeo, and Juliet (1595).

June
Pronunciation: joon
June is the sixth month of the year. The name was possibly derived from the Latin Iunius. The name is often associated with the Latin name Juno. June is known as the bridal month. June was the most successful of the names that were taken from the months of the year. The name was first adopted as a first name in the early 20th century.

Juno
Pronunciation: joo-NO
The name Juno is of Latin origin. The meaning of Juno is "queen of heaven". Borne in Roman mythology; Juna was a Roman goddess, wife, and sister of Jupiter and the queen of heaven. She is identified with the Greek goddess Hera, as patron of women and marriage.

Justine
Pronunciation: juss-Tine
The name Justine is of Latin origin. The meaning of Justine is "fair, upright". Justine is a feminine form of the masculine name Justin. Originally a French from of the Latinate name Justina. Lawrence Durrell popularised the name with his novel, Justine (1957).

K

Kacie

Pronunciation: KAY-see

The name Kacie is of American origin. The meaning of Kacie is "alert, vigorous". Kacie is a variant of the name Casey.

Kadenza

Pronunciation: KAD-en-za

The name Kadenza is of Latin origin. The meaning of Kadenza is "with rhythm".

Kady

Pronunciation: KAY-dee

The name Kady is of American origin. The meaning of Kady is unknown. Kady is a variant of the name Katy.

Kai

Pronunciation: kye

Kai is of Hawaiian origin. The meaning of the name Kai is "the sea".

Kaila

Pronunciation: KYE-lah

The name Kaila is of Hebrew and Hawaiian origin. The meaning of Kaila is "the laurel crown".

Kaitlin

Pronunciation: KAYT-len

Kaitlin is of Irish origin. The meaning of the name Kaitlin is "pure". Kaitlin is a phonetic form of the name Caitlin, an Irish form of Catherine.

Kamala

Pronunciation: KAM-al-ah

The name Kamala is of Sanskrit origin. The meaning of Kamala is "pink". Kamala is a feminine form of the masculine name Kamal. In classical Hindu texts, Kamala is a byname of the goddess of Lakshmi. The name is also borne by the wife of Shiva.

Karen

Pronunciation: KARE-en

The name Karen is of Danish origin. The meaning of the name Karen is "pure". Karen is a variation of the name Katherine. Karen became one of the most popular girls' names in Britain during the 1970's.

Kate

Pronunciation: KAY-te

The name Kate is a variation of Katherine. The name has become a popular first name by its own right.

Katherine, Katharine

Pronunciation: KATH-er-rin

Katherine is of Greek origin. The meaning of the name Katherine is "pure". Katherine is a Latin form of the name Catherine. Kathrine is the English spelling; Katharine is the Scottish spelling. The early Latin forms Katerina and Caterina became Katharine and Catherine.

Kathleen

Pronunciation: kath-LEEN

The name Kathleen is of Irish origin. The meaning of Kathleen is "pure". Kathleen is a variation of Catherine, which was influenced by the Irish Gaelic name Caítlin. The name was first used outside of Ireland in the 19th century.

Kathryn
Pronunciation: KATH-ryn
The name Kathryn is of Greek origin. The meaning of Kathryn is "pure". Kathryn is a variant of the names Catherine and Kathrine.

Katrina
Pronunciation: ka-TREE-nah
Katrina is of Greek origin. The meaning of the name Katrina is unknown. Katrina is a variation of the names Catriona and Catrina.

Katya
Pronunciation: KAT-ya
Katya is of Greek and Russian origin. The meaning of the name Katya is "pure". Katya is a Russian form of the Greek name Katherine.

Kay, Kaye
Pronunciation: kay
The name Kay is of Greek origin. The meaning of Kay is "pure". Diminutives of Katherine and Kathleen. The name became a popular first name in its own right.

Kayleigh
Pronunciation: kay-LEE
The name Kayleigh is of Irish and Gaelic origin. The meaning of Kayleigh is "slim and fair". Kayleigh is a variant of the names Cayla and Kaylee.

Kellie, Kelly
Pronunciation: KELL-ee
The name Kelly is of Irish and Gaelic origin. The meaning of Kelly is "strife, warlike". Originally an Irish surname. The name is an anglicised form of the ancient Irish Gaelic name Ceallach.

Kendall
Pronunciation: KEN-dal
The name Kendall is of Old English origin. The meaning of the name Kendall is "the Kent River Valley". An adopted surname, from a Cumbrian place name, Kendal. The name is used as both a boy's name, and as a girl's name. Kendal has been used as a given name since the 19th century.

Kerenza
Pronunciation: KER-en-za
The name Kerenza is of English origin. The meaning of Kerenza is "love, affection". Kerenza is a variant of the Cornish name Kerensa.

Kerry
Pronunciation: KARE-ee
The name Kerry is of Irish and Gaelic origin. The meaning of Kerry is "black". Kerry is also a place name of an Irish county. The name was first used by Irish immigrants to Australia for their sons. Kerry is used as both a girl's name and as a boy's name.

Khadija
Pronunciation: kah-DEE-jah
The name Khadija is of Arabic origin. The meaning of Khadija is "early baby". Khadijah bint-Khuwaylid was the first wife

of Prophet Muhammad and mother of all of his children. She was named in Koran as one of the four perfect women.

Kiara

Pronunciation: kee-AR-ah
Kiara is of Irish origin. The meaning of the name Kiara is "black". Kiara is a variant of the Irish name Ciara. The name is also a feminine form of Kieran.

Kiera

Pronunciation: kee-RAH
The name Kiera is of Irish origin. The meaning of Kiera is "black, lord". Kiera is a variant of the Irish name Ciara and is a modern feminine form of Ciaran. Kiera is also a variant of the Greek name Kira.

Kim

Pronunciation: KIM
The name Kim is of English origin. The meaning of Kim is "gold". Originally a diminutive of Kimball or Kimberley. The name is used as both a boy's name, and as a girl's name.

Kimberley

Pronunciation: KIM-ber-lee
The name Kimberley is of English origin. The meaning of Kimberley is "Cyneburg's field". Kimberley is used as both a girl's name, and as a boy's name.

Kira

Pronunciation: KEER-ah
Kira is of Greek origin. The meaning of the name Kira is "Lord". Kira is a variant of the name Kyra.

Kitty

Pronunciation: KIH-tee
The name Kitty is of Greek origin. The meaning of Kitty is "pure". Kitty is a diminutive of the Greek name Katherine. The name has been used as a first name since the 15th century. The name was also used as a slang term for a woman of dubious morals during the 17th century.

Kirsten

Pronunciation: KERS-ten
Kirsten is of Latin and Scandinavian origin. The meaning of the name Kirsten is "follower of Christ". Kirsten is a Scandinavian form of the name Christine.

Kirstie, Kirsty

Pronunciation: KERS-tee
The name Kirsty is of Scottish origin. The meaning of Kirsty is "follower of Christ". Scottish diminutives of Christina or Christine.

Kristen

Pronunciation: KRISS-ten
Kristen is of Latin origin. The meaning of the name Kristen is "follower of Christ". Kristen is a variant of Christine.

Kristin

Pronunciation: KRISS-tin
Kristin is of Latin origin. The meaning of the name Kristin is "follower of Christ".

Kristin is a variant of Christina and Christine. The name is also a feminine form of Christianus.

Kylie

Pronunciation: KYE-lee

The name Kylie is of Australian origin. The meaning of Kylie is "boomerang". The name was probably coined as a feminine form of the masculine name Kyle. The name was most popular during the 1980's. The name was made famous by Australian actress and singer, Kylie Minogue.

Kynthia

Pronunciation: kyn-THIA

The name Kynthia is of Greek origin. The meaning of Kynthia is "from Mount Kynthos". Kynthia is a variant of the Greek name Cynthia.

Kyoko

Pronunciation: kee-OH-koh

Kyoko is of Japanese origin. The meaning of the name Kyoko is "mirror".

Kyra

Pronunciation: KEER-ah

Kyra is of Greek origin. The meaning of the name Kyra is "Lord". Kyra is a feminine form of the masculine name Kyros.

L

Lacey
Pronunciation: LAY-see
Lacey is of Old French origin. The meaning of the name Lacey is unknown. Originally a nobleman's surname. The name was brought to Britain by the Normans.

Ladonna
Pronunciation: la-DAH-nah
The name Ladonna is of Italian origin. The meaning of Ladonna is "Lady". Ladonna is a modern form of the Italian name, Donna.

Laetitia
Pronunciation: le-TISH-ah
The name Laetitia is of Latin origin. The meaning of Laetitia is "joy". Diminutives: Lettie, Letty, Tisha.

Laila
Pronunciation: LAY-lah
The name Laila is of Arabic origin. The meaning of Laila is "night beauty".

Lakeisha
Pronunciation: lah-KEE-shah
Lakeisha is of uncertain origin. The meaning of the name Lakeisha is "cassia tree". Lakeisha is an elaborated form of the name Keisha.

Laine
Pronunciation: layn
The name Laine is of English origin. The meaning of Laine is "path, roadway". Laine is a variant of the surname Lane. The name is also used as a short form of the name Marlaine and Melanie.

Lainey
Pronunciation: layn-EE
The name Lainey is of French origin. The meaning of Lainey is "bright, shining light". Lainey is a diminutive of the Old French name Elaine.

Lakshmi
Pronunciation: la-KSH-mi
The name Lakshmi is of Hindi and Sanskrit origin. The meaning of Lakshmi is "good sign, good omen". Borne by the goddess of beauty, good fortune, and wealth. Lakshmi is the wife of Vishnu and the mother of Kama.

Lana
Pronunciation: LAHN-ah
Lana is of modern coinage. The name is possibly a variant of the Old German name Alana, which means "precious." American actress Lana Turner (1921-1995) popularised the name.

Lara
Pronunciation: LAR-ah
Lara is of Latin origin. The meaning of the name Lara is "protection". Lara is a diminutive of the name Larissa. Lara is also a Spanish surname and a place name. Boris Pasternak popularised the name in his novel, Dr. Zhivago (1957).

Larissa
Pronunciation: la-RISS-ah
Larissa is of Latin origin. The meaning of the name Larissa is "cheerful". The name

was borne by a Greek martyr of the Eastern Church.

Laura
Pronunciation: LAW-rah
The name Laura is of Latin origin. The meaning of Laura is "the bay, the laurel plant". Laura is a feminine form of laurus. The love poet Petrarch (1304-1374) addressed his sonnets to a Laura.

Laurel
Pronunciation: LAWR-el
The name Laurel is of Latin origin. The meaning of Laurel is "the bay, the laurel plant". A nature name derived from the name of the tree.

Lauren
Pronunciation: LAWR-en
The name Lauren is of Latin origin. The meaning of Lauren is "the bay, the laurel plant". Lauren is a variant of the name Laura. The name is also a feminine form of the masculine name Lawrence. Hollywood actress Lauren Bacall (1924-2014) popularised the name during the 20th century.

Lavinia
Pronunciation: la-vee-NEE-ah
The name Lavinia is of Latin origin. The meaning of Lavinia is unknown. Borne in mythology by the daughter of Latinus, king of the Latini. Lavinia became the wife of Aeneas and the ancestress of Romulus and Remus. The name was popular during the Renaissance and was later revived in the 18th century.

Layla
Pronunciation: LAY-la
The name Layla is of Arabic origin. The meaning of Layla is "wine". Layla is a variation of the Arabic name Leila.

Leah
Pronunciation: LAY-ah
Leah is of Hebrew origin. The meaning of the name Leah is "delicate, cow". A biblical name; borne by Jacob's first wife and the mother of Jacob's twelve sons (Genesis 29). The name was revived by the Puritans,

Leanne, Leanna
Pronunciation: lee-AN-ah
The name Leanne is of English origin. The meaning of Leanne is unknown. The name is either a combination of the name Lee and Anna or possibly a variation of the name Liane.

Leanora
Pronunciation: LEE-nor-ah
The name Leanora is of Italian origin. The meaning of Leanora is "compassion, light". Leanore is the Italian form the Old German name Eleanor.

Leda
Pronunciation: LEE-dah
The name Leda is of Greek origin. The meaning of Leda is "joy, happiness". Borne in Greek mythology; Leda was the Queen of

Sparta and the mother of Helen of Troy and Clytemnestra.

Lee

Pronunciation: LEE

Lee is of Old English origin. The meaning of the name Lee is "wood, meadow, clearing". An adopted surname and place name. Lee was first used as a first name in the 19th century, probably in honour of the Confederate general Robert E. Lee (1807-1870). The name is used as both a boy's name, and as a girl's name.

Leila

Pronunciation: LEE-lah

The name Leila is of Arabic origin. The meaning of Leila is "night beauty".

Lena

Pronunciation: LEE-nah

The name Lena is originally a byname from female names ending in –lena, such as Helena. The name became a popular first name in its own right.

Leona

Pronunciation: LEE-oh-nah

Leona is of Latin origin. The meaning of the name Leona is "Lion". Leona is a feminine form of the masculine name Leon.

Leonie

Pronunciation: LEE-oh-nee

Leonie is of Latin origin. The meaning of the name Leonie is "Lion". Leonie is a feminine form of the masculine name Leon. Leonie is the French form.

Leonora

Pronunciation: lee-a-NOR-ah

The name Leonora is of Greek and Italian origin. The meaning of Leonora is "compassion, light". Leonora is the Italian form of the name Eleanor. Beethoven popularised the name is his opera Fidelio (1814). Diminutives: Leo, Nora, Norah.

Lesley

Pronunciation: les-LEE

The name Lesley is of Scottish origin. The meaning of Lesley is "Holly Garden". Originally a Scottish surname derived from a place called Lesslyn in Aberdeenshire. Lesley is a variant of the name Leslie.

Liesel

Pronunciation: LIE-sel

The name Liesel is German and Hebrew origin. The meaning of Liesel is "God is my oath". Liesel is a German diminutive of the name Elizabeth.

Lili

Pronunciation: LIL-ee

Lili is of German and Hebrew origin. The meaning of the name Lili is "lily; God is my oath". Lili is a German diminutive of the name Elizabeth. The name became a popular first name in its own right.

Lilian

Pronunciation: LIL-e-an

The name Lilian is of Latin origin. The meaning of Lilian is "lily". Lilian is also a variant of the name Lily. Diminutives: Lily.

Lily
Pronunciation: LIL-ee
Lily is of Greek and Latin origin. The meaning of the name Lily is "lily". From Greek leirion, which denotes a species of slender plants with trumpet-shaped flowers. The lily is a symbol of innocence and purity. The name became popular during the 19th century when botanical names became fashionable.

Lina
Pronunciation: LY-na
The name Lina is of Arabic and Latin origin. The meaning of Lina is "palm tree". Lina is a diminutive of names that end with -lina, such as Selina.

Linda
Pronunciation: LIN-dah
The name Linda is of Spanish origin. The meaning of Linda is "pretty". Linda is also a byname for the names Belinda and Melinda. Diminutives: Lin, Lindie, Lindy.

Lindsay
Pronunciation: LIN-d-say
Lindsay is of Old English origin. The meaning of the name Lindsay is "Lincoln's marsh". Sir Walter de Lindesay brought the name to Scotland from Lindsey, Lincolnshire. The name is used as both a boy's name and as a girl's name.

Lisa
Pronunciation: LEE-sah
Lisa is of Hebrew origin. The meaning of the name Lisa is "God is my oath". Lisa is a variation of the name Liza. The name was popular throughout the 20th century.

Livia
Pronunciation: LIV-iah
Livia is of Latin origin. The meaning of the name Livia is "olive, tree". Livia is a feminine form of the Roman clan name Livius.

Lois
Pronunciation: LOH-iss
The name Lois is of Greek origin. The meaning of Lois is "superior". A biblical name; borne in the New Testament by the grandmother of Timothy.

Lola
Pronunciation: LOH-lah
The name Lola is of unknown origin. The meaning of Lola is "sorrows". Lola is a Spanish diminutive of the name Dolores.

Lolita
Pronunciation: LOH-e-tah
The name Lolita is of unknown origin. The meaning of Lolita is "sorrows". Lolita is a Spanish diminutive of the name Dolores.

Lorna
Pronunciation: LOR-nah
The name Lorna is of Scottish origin. The meaning of Lorna is unknown. The name was invented by R.D Blackmore for his novel Lorna Doone (1869). The name was

possibly derived from an area of Argyll; Scotland called Lorne.

Lorraine
Pronunciation: lor-AYN
The name Lorraine is of French origin. The meaning of Lorraine is "from Lorraine". Originally an adopted French surname derived from the district of Alsace-Lorraine.

Louisa
Pronunciation: LOH-e-sah
The name Louisa is of Latin origin. The meaning of Louisa is "famous warrior". Louisa is the Latinate feminine form of the name Louis. The name was popular during the 17th century. Diminutives: Lou, Louie, Lulu.

Louise
Pronunciation: loo-EEZ
The name Louise is of Old German and French origin. The meaning of Louise is "famous warrior". Louise is a French feminine form of the masculine name Louis. Saint Louise (16th century) was the co-founder of the nursing order Daughter of Charity. The name was adopted in Britain during the 17th century. Diminutives: Lou, Louie, Lulu.

Lucia
Pronunciation: LOU-cee-ah
Lucia is of Italian and Latin origin. The meaning of the name Lucia is "light". Lucia is a feminine form of the Latin name Lucius.

Lucilla
Pronunciation: LOO-sil-lah
The name Lucilla is of Latin origin. The meaning of Lucilla is "light". Lucilla is a Latin byname for Lucia. The name was borne by several saints. The name was popular with the Romans and later revived in the 19th century.

Lucille
Pronunciation: loo-SEEL
Lucille is of French origin. The meaning of Lucille is "light". Lucille is the French form. The name was made popular by American actress Lucille Ball (1911-1989).

Lucinda
Pronunciation: loo-SEEN-dah
The name Lucinda is of Latin origin. The meaning of Lucinda is "light". Lucinda is a variant of the Latin name Lucy.

Lucy
Pronunciation: LOO-see
The name Lucy is of Latin origin. The meaning of Lucy is "light". Lucy is an anglicised form of the Old French name Lucie. The name is borne by a fourth-century saint. Saint Lucy is the patroness of sight. Diminutives: Loose, Luce.

Lulu
Pronunciation: LOO-loo
The name Lulu is of Spanish and German origin. The meaning of Lulu is "famous warrior". Lulu is a byname of Luisa, Luise,

and Louise. The name became a popular first name in its own right.

Lydia
Pronunciation: LED-ee-ah
The name Lydia is of Greek origin. The meaning of Lydia is "woman of Lydia, from Lydia", a town in Asia Minor. A biblical name; borne by a woman who was converted to Christianity by Saint Paul (16:14).

Lyn, Lynn
Pronunciation: lyn
The name Lyn is of uncertain origin. The meaning of Lyn is "pretty". Lyn is a variant of the name Linda.

Lynette
Pronunciation: le-NET
The name Lynette is of Welsh origin. The meaning of Lynette is "idol, nymph". Originally adopted from the medieval French form of Eluned. Lord Tennyson (1859-1885) popularised the modern form of the name in Idylls of the King.

Lyra
Pronunciation: LY-rah
The name Lyra is of Greek origin. The meaning of Lyra is "lyre". Lyra is a variant of the Greek name Lyris.

M

Mackenzie
Pronunciation: ma-KEN-zee
The name Mackenzie if of Gaelic and Irish origin. The meaning of Mackenzie is "son of the wise ruler". An adopted Scottish surname, from Gaelic Mac Coinnich. Mackenzie is used as both a boy's name, and as a girl's name.

Madelaine
Pronunciation: MAD-el-aine
The name Madelaine is of French and Hebrew origin. The meaning of Madelaine is "woman from Magdala". Magdala is a village by the Sea of Galilee. Madelaine is a medieval French form of the name Magdalene.

Magdalen, Magdalene
Pronunciation: MAG-da-len
The name Magdalen is of Hebrew origin. The meaning of Magdalen is "woman from Magdala". Magdala is a village by the Sea of Galilee. A biblical name; borne by Saint Mary Magdalene, a reformed prostitute, and follower of Jesus.

Mahalia
Pronunciation: ma-HAL-yah
The name Mahalia is of Hebrew origin. The meaning of Mahalia is "tenderness".

Maia, Maya
Pronunciation: MA-ia
Maia is of Greek origin. The meaning of the name Maia is "great, mother". Maia is a variation of the name Mary. Borne in Greek mythology; Maia was a beautiful nymph and mother of Hermes. In Roman mythology, she is the eldest and most beautiful of the Pleiades. The month of May was named in honour of her. In Buddhist philosophy, Maya gave birth to Buddha in the shape of a little white elephant.

Mallory
Pronunciation: MALL-or-ee
The name Mallory is of Old French origin. The meaning of Mallory is "unfortunate". The name is used as both a boy's name, and as a girl's name.

Márie
Pronunciation: mar-EE
The name Márie is of Irish Gaelic origin. The meaning of Márie is unknown.

Maisie
Pronunciation: MAY-zee
Maisie if of English origin. The meaning of the name Maisie is "pearl". Maisie is a diminutive of the names Margaret, Marjorie, and Mary.

Manon
Pronunciation: MAN-awn
The name Manon is of French origin. The meaning of Man is "star of the sea". Manon is a French diminutive of the name Marie.

Manuela
Pronunciation: mahn-WAY-lah
The name Manuela is of Spanish and Hebrew origin. The meaning of Manuela is "God is with us". Manuela is a feminine form of the name Manuel.

Mara, Marah
Pronunciation: MAHR-ah
The name Mara is of Hebrew origin. The meaning of Mara is "bitter". A biblical name; adopted by Naomi, mother-in-law of Ruth. She claimed the name Mara after the death of her husband and sons.

Marcella, Marcelle
Pronunciation: mar-SELL-ah
Marcella is of Latin origin. The meaning of the name Marcella is "dedicated to Mars". Marcella is a feminine form of a Roman family name Marcellus. Marcelle is the French form. Saint Marcella from the 4th century was killed during the sack of Rome.

Marcia
Pronunciation: MAR-shah
Marcia is of Latin origin. The meaning of the name Marcia is "dedicated to Mars". Marcia is a feminine form of the Roman family name Marcius. Diminutives: Marcie, Marcy.

Maretta
Pronunciation: mar-ee-et-AH
The name Maretta is of Scottish origin. The meaning of Maretta is "star of the sea". Maretta is an anglicised form of Mairead and the Scottish Gaelic form of the name Margaret.

Margaret
Pronunciation: MARG-ar-et
The name Margaret is of Greek origin. The meaning of Margaret is "pearl". Derived from the Latin name, Margarita, which was derived from Greek margaron. Saint Margaret of Antioch was a 3rd-century virgin martyr, is renowned for fighting the devil in the shape of a dragon. Diminutives: Daisy, Madge, Maggie, Marge, Margie, Margy, Marji, Marjie, May, Meg, Meggie, Peg, Peggy.

Margarita
Pronunciation: MARG-ar-ee-TAH
The name Margarita is of Spanish origin. The meaning of Margarita is "pearl". Margarita is a Spanish form of Margaret. The name became a popular first name in its own right.

Margherita
Pronunciation: MARG-er-ee-TAH
The name Margherita is of Italian origin. The meaning of Margherita is "pearl". Margherita is an Italian form of Margaret. The name became a popular first name in its own right.

Marguerite
Pronunciation: mar-gue-rite
The name Marguerite is of French origin. The meaning of Marguerite is "pearl". Marguerite is French variation of the name Margaret. The name was first adopted during the 19th century. Diminutives: Margot.

Maria
Pronunciation: mah-REE-ah
Maria is of Latin origin. The meaning of the name Maria is "star of the sea". Maria is the Latinate form of the name Mary. The name

was revived during the 20th century, possibly due to the popularity of the American musical, West Side Story.

Mariah
Pronunciation: mah-ri-AH
Mariah is of Latin origin. The meaning of the name Mariah is "star of the sea". Mariah is a variant of the name Maria. The name dates back to the 19th century. The name was popularised by American singer Mariah Carey.

Marian
Pronunciation: mar-ee-AHN
The name Marian is of French origin. The meaning of Marian is "star of the sea". Marian is a French diminutive of the name Marie. The name became a popular first name during the Middle Ages. The name was later revived in the 19th century.

Marie
Pronunciation: mah-REE
The name Marie is of French origin. The meaning of Marie is "star of the sea". Marie is a French form of the Latin name Maria. The name became a popular first name in its own right.

Mariella
Pronunciation: mar-EE-el-AH
Mariella is of German origin. The meaning of the name Mariella is "star of the sea". Mariella is originally a German diminutive of the name Mary.

Marietta
Pronunciation: MAR-e-ett-AH
The name Marietta is of Italian origin. The meaning of Marietta is "star of the sea". Marietta is an Italian diminutive of the name Mary. Mariette is the French form.

Marilyn
Pronunciation: MARE-a-lin
Marilyn is of English origin. The meaning of the name Marilyn is "star of the sea". Marilyn is a variation of the name Mary. The name was popularised in the 20th century by Hollywood actress Marilyn Monroe (1926-1962).

Marina
Pronunciation: mah-REE-nag
The name Marina is of Latin origin. The meaning of Marina is "from the sea". Possibly derived from Latin Marinus, or from a Latin family name that is related to Marius. The name was borne by the 14th-century martyr of the Greek Church. Shakespeare used the name in Pericles, Prince of Tyre (1619).

Marissa
Pronunciation: ma-RISS-ah
The name Marissa is of Latin origin. The meaning of Marissa is "of the sea", Marissa is a diminutive of the name Mary.

Marlene
Pronunciation: mar-LEEN
The name Marlene is of German origin. The meaning of Marlene is "star of the sea". The name was introduced to Britain

by Lili Marlene. German and Hollywood actress Marlene Dietrich (1901-1992) popularised the name during the 20th century.

Marnie

Pronunciation: marn-EE

Marnie is of Scandinavian origin. The meaning of the name Marnie is "from the sea". Marnie is a variant of the Latin name, Marina. The name is also a diminutive of Marna.

Martha

Pronunciation: MAR-tha

Martha is of Aramaic origin. The meaning of the name Martha is "Lady". A biblical name; borne in the New Testament by the sister of Lazarus and Mary of Bethany. She is the patron saint of the helping professions. The name was revived by the Puritans.

Martina, Martine

Pronunciation: mar-TEEN-ah

The name Martina is of Latin origin. The meaning of Martina is "dedicated to Mars". Martina is a feminine form of the masculine name Martin. Martina is the Latinate form; Martine is the French form. The name was borne by two saints.

Mary

Pronunciation: MARE-ee

The name Mary is of Latin origin. The meaning of the name Mary is "star of the sea". Mary is a medieval Anglicisation of the French name Marie. A biblical name; borne by the virgin mother of Christ, Mary became the object of great worship in the Catholic Church. Mary Magdalene and Mary of Bethany are also mentioned in the Bible. Diminutives: Maidie, Maisie, Mamie, May, Mimi, Minnie, Moll, Molly, Poll, Polly.

Matilda

Pronunciation: mah-TIL-dah

The name Matilda is of Old German origin. The meaning of Matilda is "mighty in battle, strength". From Old German mahti. The name was introduced to Britain in the 11th century by Queen Matilda, wife of William the Conqueror. Diminutives: Mattie, Matty, Tilda, Tilly.

May

Pronunciation: may

The name May is of English origin. The meaning of May is "the fifth month". The name is derived from the Latin Maius. May is one of the names of the months that were adopted as first names in the early 20th century. May is a diminutive of the name Mary.

Maybelle

Pronunciation: MAY-belle

The name Maybelle is of English origin. The meaning of Maybelle is "lovable". Maybelle is a variant of the English name Mabel.

Maxine

Pronunciation: mak-SEEN

The name Maxine if of Latin origin. The meaning of Maxine is "greatest". Maxine if a feminine form of the name Max.

Megan
Pronunciation: MEG-an
Megan is of Welsh origin. The meaning of the name Megan is "pearl". Megan is a Welsh diminutive of Meg.

Mehetabel
Pronunciation: meh-et-a-bel
The name Mehetabel is of Hebrew origin. The meaning of Mehetabel is "God makes happy". A biblical name; borne by a figure mentioned in the Old Testament.

Melanie
Pronunciation: MEL-a-nee
The name Melanie is of French and Greek origin. The meaning of Melanie is "black, dark". The name is derived from the French form of the Latin name Melania. The name is borne by two Roman saints. The name was introduced to Britain in the 17th century. Margaret Mitchell popularised the name in her epic novel, Gone With The Wind (1936). Melanie Wilkes is the wife of Ashely Wilkes and Scarlet O' Hara's best friend.

Melba
Pronunciation: MEL-bah
The name Melba is of Australian origin. The name is derived from the Australian place name Melbourne. The name was possibly created as a surname by Diva Nellie Melba (1861-1931).

Melinda
Pronunciation: ma-LIN-dah
The name Melinda is of Latin origin. The meaning of Melinda is "sweet". The name is an 18th-century coinage, a combination of the names Mel and Linda. The name was also influenced by the Greek name Melissa and is often associated with bees, honey, and sweetness.

Melissa
Pronunciation: ma-LISS-ah
Melissa is of Greek origin. The meaning of the name Melissa is "bee, honey". Borne in Greek mythology by a princess of Crete, who introduced mankind to honey.
Diminutives: Mel.

Melody
Pronunciation: MEL-a-dee
The name Melody is of Greek origin. The meaning of Melody is "song, music". Melody is a direct adoption from the English vocabulary, which denotes a musical tune. The name was first used in the 13th century.

Mercedes
Pronunciation: mer-SAY-dees
Mercedes is of Spanish origin. The meaning of the name Mercedes is "mercies". Derived from Maria de Las Mercedes, a Spanish title for the Virgin Mary. Mercedes is also the name of the German luxury car.
Diminutives: Mercy, Sadie.

Mercy
Pronunciation: MER-see
Mercy is of English origin. The meaning of the name Mercy is "compassion". The name is a direct adaptation from the English vocabulary. The virtue name was adopted by the Puritans in the 17th century. Mercy is also a diminutive of the name Mercedes.

Merlin
Pronunciation: MER-lin
Merlin is of Welsh origin. The meaning of the name Melvin is "sea fortress". From the Latinate form, Merlinus, of the Old Welsh name Myrddin. Borne in Arthurian legend by magician Merlin Ambrosius. The name is used as both a boy's name, and as a girl's name.

Mia
Pronunciation: MEE-ah
Mia is of Latin and Scandinavian origin. The meaning of the name Mia is "star of the sea". Mia is a Scandinavian diminutive of the Latin name Maria. The name was popularised in the 20th century by Hollywood actress Mia Farrow.

Michaela
Pronunciation: mih-KAY-lah
The name Michaela is of Hebrew origin. The meaning of Michaela is "who is like God." Michaela is a feminine form of the masculine name Michael.

Michelle
Pronunciation: mee-SHELL
Michelle is of French and Hebrew origin. The meaning of the name Michelle is "who is like God." Michelle is a feminine form of the French name Michel. The name was popularised by the Beatles in the 20th century. Diminutives: Chelle, Mich, Michy, Shell, Shelley, Shelly.

Mignon
Pronunciation: mig-NON
The name Mignon is of French origin. The meaning of Mignon is "cute, dainty".

Millie, Milly
Pronunciation: mill-EE
Millie is of Latin and Old German origin. The meaning of Millie is "rival, bee, honey". Millie is a diminutive of the names Camila, Mildred, and Millicent.

Mimi
Pronunciation: MEE-mee
Mimi is of French origin. The meaning of the name Mimi is "star of the sea". Mimi is a diminutive of the name Mary.

Mina
Pronunciation: MEE-nah
The name Mina is of German origin. The meaning of the name Mina is "love". Mina is a diminutive of the names Philomena and Wilhelmina.

Minerva
Pronunciation: mi-NER-vah
The name Minerva is of Latin origin. The meaning of Minerva is "the mind". Borne in mythology; Minerva was the Roman

goddess of wisdom, arts, crafts and war. She is equivalent to the Greek goddess Athena.

Minna
Pronunciation: min-NAH
The name Minna is of Old German origin. The meaning of Minna is "determined protector". Minna is a diminutive of the name Wilhelmina.

Minnie
Pronunciation: min-EE
Minnie is of uncertain origin. The meaning of Minnie is "star of the sea, determined protector". Minnie is a diminutive of the names Mary and Wilhelmina. The name became a popular first name in its own right. Walt Disney popularised the name in the 20th century, by using it for the name of Mickey Mouse's girlfriend.

Mirabella
Pronunciation: mira-bel-LAH
The name Mirabella is of Latin origin. The meaning of Mirabella is "wonderful". The name was popular in medieval Britain.

Miranda
Pronunciation: mer-ANN-dah
The name Miranda is of Latin origin. The meaning of Miranda is "worthy of admiration". The name was used by Shakespeare in The Tempest (1612). Miranda was the name of the innocent heroine, raised and educated on an isolated island by her magician father.

Miriam
Pronunciation: MEER-ee-em
The name Miriam is of Hebrew origin. The meaning of Miriam is "star of the sea". Miriam is an old-fashioned form of the name Mary. A biblical name; borne by the sister of Moses and Aaron. The name was adopted by the Puritans. The name was later revived in the 18th century.

Mitzi
Pronunciation: MIT-zee
Mitzi is of German origin. The meaning of the name Mitzi is "star of the sea". Mitzi is originally a German diminutive of the Latin name Maria.

Modesty
Pronunciation: MAH-dess-tee
The name Modesty is of Latin origin. The meaning of Modesty is "modest, without conceit". Modesty is a virtue name.

Mohana
Pronunciation: mo-HAN-ah
The name Mohana is of Sanskrit origin. The meaning of Mohana is "attractive, enchanting".

Moira
Pronunciation: MOY-rah
The name Moira is of English origin. The meaning of Moira is "star of the sea". Moria is the Irish Gaelic form of the name Mary.

Moll
Pronunciation: moll

The name Moll is of Latin origin. The meaning of Moll is “star of the sea”. Moll is a diminutive of the names Mary and Molly.

Molly
Pronunciation: moll-EE
The name Molly is of Latin origin. The meaning of Molly is “star of the sea”. Molly is a diminutive of the names Mary.

Mona
Pronunciation: MOH-nah
The name Mona is of Irish Gaelic origin. The meaning of Mona is “aristocratic, noble”. Mona is an anglicised form of the Irish Gaelic name Muadhnait. Mona is sometimes used as a diminutive of the name Monica. The name is also an Italian short form of the name, Madonna. Leonardo da Vinci popularised the name with his famous painting, Mona Lisa.

Monica
Pronunciation: MAH-ni-kah
Monica is of Latin origin. The meaning of the name Monica is “advisor, alone”. Borne by the mother of Saint Augustine, she prayed for her son and saved him from self-destruction. American sitcom, Friends (1994-2004) popularised the name with its character Monica Geller.

Monique
Pronunciation: mon-EEK
The name Monique is of French and Latin origin. The meaning of Monique is “advisor”. Monique is the French form of the Latin name Monica.

Morwenna
Pronunciation: mor-WEN-ah
The name Morwenna is of Welsh origin. The meaning of Morwenna is “maiden”. The name is borne by a 5th-century Cornish saint.

Myra
Pronunciation: MYE-rah
The name Myra is of Greek origin. The meaning of the name Myra is “myrrh”. The name was a poetic and literary invention by the English poet Fulke Greville (1554-1628). The name was popular during the 19th century.

N

Nadia
Pronunciation: NAH-d'-yah
The name Nadia is of Russian origin. The meaning of Nadia is "hope". The name is an Anglicisation of Nadya, diminutive of the Russian name Nadezhda. The name is popular in Russia.

Nadine
Pronunciation: nay-DEEN
Nadine is of Russian origin. The meaning of the name Nadine is unknown. The name is a French diminutive of Nadia. The name was first used in the 20th century when Diaghilev's Ballets Russes was established in Paris.

Naida
Pronunciation: NAY-da
The name Naida is of Greek origin. The meaning of Naida is "water nymph".

Nancy
Pronunciation: NAN-cee
Nancy is of Hebrew origin. The meaning of the name Nancy is "grace". The name is originally a diminutive of the name Constance. However, during the 18th century, the name was regarded as a diminutive of Anne. Diminutives: Nan, Nance.

Naomh
Pronunciation: nay-OHM
The name Naomh is of Irish Gaelic origin. The meaning of the Naomh is "holy".

Naomi
Pronunciation: nay-OH-mee
The name Naomi is of Hebrew origin. The meaning of Naomi is "pleasant". A biblical name; borne in the Old Testament an ancestress of Jesus and mother in law to Ruth. The name has long been popular with Jewish families.

Natalia, Natalya
Pronunciation: NAT-al-ee-a
Natalia is of Russian origin. The meaning of the name Natalia is "birthday". Derived from Latin natale domini. The name refers to the birthday of Christ. Saint Natalia was Saint Adrian's wife. Diminutives: Talia, Talya, Tally.

Natalie
Pronunciation: NAT-a-lee
The name Natalie is of Latin origin. The meaning of Natalie is "birthday". The name is a French form of Natalya. The name dates back to the 20th century when Diaghilev's Ballet Russes was first established in Paris.

Natasha
Pronunciation: na-TAH-shah
The name Natasha is of Russian origin. The meaning of Natasha is "birthday". Natasha is a diminutive of the name Natalya. The name became a popular first name in its own right. The name became famous with Leo Tolstoy's epic novel War and Peace (1865-9). Natasha was the name of the heroine. Diminutives: Tash, Tasha.

Neila
Pronunciation: NEE-lah

The name Neila is of Hebrew origin. The meaning of Neila is "closing". The name is a feminine form of the masculine name Neil.

Nelinia

Pronunciation: NEL-ee-nee-a

The name Nelinia is of Scottish origin. The meaning of Nelinia is "Champion". Nelinina is a feminine form of the masculine name Neil.

Neima

Pronunciation: NEE-ma

The name Neima is of Hebrew origin. The meaning of Neima is "melody".

Neiva

Pronunciation: NEE-vah

The name Neiva is of Spanish origin. The meaning of Neiva is "snow". Neiva is a feminine variant of the word, nieve.

Neka

Pronunciation: NEE-ka

The name Neka is of Native American Indian origin. The meaning of Neka is "wild goose".

Nelia

Pronunciation: NEE-lee-a

Nelia is of Latin origin. The meaning of the name Nelia is "horn". Nelia is a diminutive of the Latin name Cornelia.

Nell

Pronunciation: N-ell

The name Nell is a diminutive of the Old French & Old German name, Eleanor. The meaning of the name Nell is "horn, sun ray". Nell can also be a variant for the names Helen, Ellen, and Nelly.

Diminutives: Nellie, Nelly.

Nelly

Pronunciation: NEL-ee

Nelly is of English origin. The meaning of the name Nelly is "sun ray". Nelly is a diminutive of the names Helen and Eleanor.

Nemera

Pronunciation: NEM-er-a

The name Nemera is of Hebrew origin. The meaning of Nemera is "leopard".

Neneca

Pronunciation: NE-ne-KA

The name Neneca is of Spanish origin. The meaning of Neneca is "industrious". Neneca is a variant of the Old German name Amelia.

Neoma

Pronunciation: NE-oo-ma

The name Neoma is of Greek origin. The meaning of Neoma is "new moon".

Nera

Pronunciation: NEE-ra

The name Nera is of Hebrew origin. The meaning of Nera is "candle".

Nereida

Pronunciation: ne-RAY-dah

Nereida is of Greek and Spanish origin. The meaning of the name Nereida is "sea nymph". Borne in Greek mythology; the Nereids were mermaids of the sea.

Nerissa
Pronunciation: NEE-riss-a
The name Nerissa is of Italian origin. The meaning of the name Nerissa is "black haired".

Nerola
Pronunciation: NE-rol-a
The name Nerola is of Italian origin. The meaning of Nerola is "orange flower".

Nerys
Pronunciation: NER-iss
The name Nerys is of Welsh origin. The meaning of Nerys is "noblewoman".

Nessa
Pronunciation: NESS-a
The name Nessa is of Scottish Gaelic origin. The meaning of Nessa is unknown. Nessa is a diminutive of the Greek name Agnes. The name was borne in Scottish legend by the mother of Conchobhar. Nessa is also used as a variant of the Greek name Vanessa.

Nettie
Pronunciation: NEH-tee
The name Nettie is of English origin. The meaning of Nettie is unknown. Nettie is a diminutive of all girls' names ending –net.

Niamh
Pronunciation: NI-amh
The name Niamh is of Irish Gaelic origin. The meaning of Niamh is "brightness". Borne in Irish mythology by the lover of Oisín, was carried off to the land of eternal youth.

Nicola
Pronunciation: NIC-o-la
Nicola is of Greek origin. The meaning of the name Nicola is "people of victory". The name is a Latinate and Italian feminine form of the name Nicholas. Diminutives: Nic, Nik, Nicki, Nicky, Niki, Nikki, Nico.

Nicole
Pronunciation: ni-KOHL
The name Nicole is of Greek origin. The meaning of Nicole is "people of victory". The name is a French feminine form of the name Nicholas.

Nigella
Pronunciation: NI-gel-la
The name Nigella is of English origin. The meaning of Nigella is "Champion". Nigella is a Latinate feminine form of the name Nigel.

Nikita
Pronunciation: nih-KEE-tah
Nikita is of Greek origin. The meaning of the name Nikita is "unconquered". Nikita is a Russian masculine name, derived from the Greek name Aniketos. The name was borne by an early pope. The name is regarded as a girl's name in the English-speaking world; however, it is still in use as a boy's name in Russia.

Nina
Pronunciation: NEE-nah
The name Nina is of Spanish and Hebrew origin. The meaning of Nina is "little girl". The name was originally a diminutive of girls' names that ended with –nina. The name became a popular first name in its own right. Christopher Columbus named one of his three ships Nina. Diminutive: Ninka.

Nisha
Pronunciation: NEE-shah
The name Nisha is of Hindi origin. The meaning of Nisha is "night",

Nissa
Pronunciation: NISS-a
The name Nissa is of Hebrew origin. The meaning of Nissa is "to test".

Nixie
Pronunciation: NIX-ee
The name Nixie is of Old German origin. The meaning of the name Nixie is "water sprite".

Noelani
Pronunciation: no-ah-LAH-nee
The name Noelani is of Hawaiian origin. The meaning of Noelani is "mist of heaven".

Noelle
Pronunciation: noe-ELL
Noelle is of Old French origin. The meaning of the name Noelle is "Christmas". Noelle is a feminine form of the name, Noel.

Nokomis
Pronunciation: n(o)-KO-mis
The name Nokomis if of Native American Indian origin. The meaning of Nokomis is "daughter of the moon".

Nolan
Pronunciation: NO-lan
The name Nolan is of Irish and Gaelic origin. The meaning of Nolan is "Champion". Nolan is an adopted surname.

Nona
Pronunciation: NOH-nah
The name Nona is of Latin origin. The meaning of Nona is "ninth". The name was originally given to a family's ninth baby.

Nora
Pronunciation: NOR-ah
Nora is of English origin. The meaning of the name Nora is "woman of honor". In Scotland, Nora is used as a feminine form of the name Norman.

Nordica
Pronunciation: NOR-dic-a
The name Nordica is of Latin origin. The meaning of Nordica is "from the North".

Noreen
Pronunciation: nor-EEN

The name Noreen is of Irish origin. The meaning of Noreen is unknown. Noreen is a variant of the name Nora.

Norell
Pronunciation: no-RELL
The name Norell is of Scandinavian origin. The meaning of Norell is "from the North". The name is originally a surname.

Norma
Pronunciation: NOR-mah
Norma is of Latin origin. The meaning of the name Norma is "the standard, norm". The name was possibly invented by Felice Romani. The name became popular in the 19th century, after Vincenzo Bellini's 1832 tragic opera, Norma. The name was popularised by Hollywood actress Norma Jeane Mortenson, also known as Marilyn Monroe (1926-1962).

Nova
Pronunciation: NOH-vah
The name Nova is of Latin origin. The meaning of Nova is "new". In astronomy, a nova is a star that releases bursts of energy.

Nuala
Pronunciation: NOO-la
The name Nuala is of Irish origin. The meaning of Nuala is unknown. The name was originally a diminutive of Fionnuala. The name is now widely used as a first name in its own its own right.

Nura
Pronunciation: NOOR-ah
The name Nura is of Arabic and Aramaic origin. The meaning of Nura is "light".

Nydia
Pronunciation: NIH-dee-ah
The name Nydia is of Latin origin. The meaning of Nydia is "nest". Taken from the word nidus. The name was popularised by Edward Bulwer-Lytton's epic novel, The Last Days of Pompeii (1834). Nydia was the name of a blind woman who died whilst saving her beloved one.

Nyna
Pronunciation: NEE-nah
The name Nyna is of English origin. The meaning of the name Nyna is unknown. Nyna is a feminine form of Nyles.

Nyree
Pronunciation: ny-REE
The name Nyree is of Maori origin. The meaning of the Nyree is unknown. The name dates back to before Christ.

Nysa
Pronunciation: NY-sa
The name Nysa is of Greek origin. The meaning of Nysa is "ambition".

Oceana
Pronunciation: oh-see-AH-nah
The name Oceana is of Greek origin. The meaning of Oceana is "ocean". The name is a feminine form of Oceanus.

Octavia
Pronunciation: ock-TAHV-yah
The name Octavia is of Latin origin. The meaning of Octavia is "eighth". The name is a feminine form of Octavius, from Latin octavus. Octavia was sometimes given to the eighth child or daughter.

Odele
Pronunciation: OH-del
The name Odele is of Greek origin. The meaning of Odele is "song". The name is also possibly a variant of Adele.

Odelia
Pronunciation: oh-DEEL-yah
The name Odelia is of Hebrew origin. The meaning of Odelia is "praise God". Borne by an 8th-century French saint.

Odessa
Pronunciation: oh-DESS-ah
The name Odessa is of Greek origin. The meaning of Odessa is "long journey". The name is a variant of Odysseus.

Odila
Pronunciation: oh-DIL-a
The name Odila is of Old German origin. The meaning of Odila is "fortunate in battle".

Ofra
Pronunciation: OF-ra
The name Ofra is of Hebrew origin. The meaning of Ofra is "fawn". The name is a variant of Ophrah.

Oksana
Pronunciation: OK-sana
The name Oksana is of Hebrew and Russian origin. The meaning of Oksana is "praise God".

Ola
Pronunciation: Oh-lah
The name Ola is of Old Norse origin. The meaning of Ola is "ancestor's relic". Ola is a variant of the Greek name Olesia.

Oleisa
Pronunciation: oh-LEE-sa
Oleisa is of French origin. The meaning of the name Oleisa is "God is my oath". Oleisa is a variant of the Hebrew name Elizabeth.

Olena
Pronunciation: oh-LEE-na
The name Olena is of Greek and Russian origin. The meaning of the name Olena is "sun ray". The name is a variant of Helen.

Olesia
Pronunciation: OL-ee-SEE-a
Olesia is of Greek origin. The meaning of the name Olesia is "man's defender".

Olethea
Pronunciation: oh-lee-THEE-ah

The name Olethea is of Greek origin. The meaning of Olethea is "truth". Olethea is a variant of the Greek name Alethea.

Olga
Pronunciation: OL-gah
The name Olga is of Old Norse and Scandinavian origin. The meaning of Olga is "blessed, holy". The name is a Russian form of Helga. Saint Olga was a 10th century Christian and Princess from Kiev.

Olina
Pronunciation: oh-LEE-nah
The name Olina is of Hawaiian origin. The meaning of Olina is "joyous".

Olinda
Pronunciation: oh-LIN-dah
The name Olinda is of Greek origin. The meaning of Olinda is "wild fig".

Olivia
Pronunciation: oh-LIV-ee-ah
The name Olivia is of Latin origin. The meaning of Olivia is "olive tree". The name is possibly a Latinate feminine form of the name, Oliver. The name was used by Shakespeare in his play Twelfth Night (1602). Saint Olivia was venerated in Italy as patron the saint of olive trees.

Olwen
Pronunciation: OL-wen
The name Olwen is of Welsh origin. The meaning of Olwen is "white footprint". Borne in the medieval story of Culhwch and Olwen, Olwen was so beautiful that wherever she stepped, four white flowers would suddenly appear.

Olympia
Pronunciation: oh-LIM-pee-ah
Olympia is of Greek origin. The meaning of the name Olympia is "from Mount Olympus". The name is a modern adaptation of the ancient name, Peloponnesus, which was the site of the early Olympic games.

Ondine
Pronunciation: ON-dine
The name Ondine is of Latin origin. The meaning of Ondine is "little wave".

Ondrea
Pronunciation: ON-dree-ah
The name Ondrea is of Czechoslovakian origin. The meaning of Ondrea is unknown. Ondrea is a variant of the name Andrea.

Oneida
Pronunciation: ON-ee-da
The name Oneida is of Native American Indian origin. The meaning of Oneida is "long-awaited".

Onella
Pronunciation: ON-el-la
The name Onella is of Greek origin. The meaning of Onella is "light".

Oona
Pronunciation: OO-nah

The name Oona is of Irish and Scottish origin. The meaning of Oona is "one". The name is an anglicised form of the Irish Gaelic name Úna.

Opal
Pronunciation: OH-pel
The name Opal is of Hindi and Sanskrit origin. The meaning of Opal is "gem". Opal is a type of semi-precious stone. The gemstone is suitable for a baby born in October. Opals have been associated with bad luck for centuries.

Ophelia
Pronunciation: oh-FEEL-yah
The name Ophelia is of Greek origin. The meaning of Ophelia is "help". Ophelia is a feminine form of Greek ophelos. Shakespeare used the name in his play, Hamlet (1601). Ophelia was the ill-fated lover of Hamlet. The name was popular during the 19th century.

Ophrah
Pronunciation: OHF-rah
Ophrah is of Hebrew origin. The meaning of the name Ophrah is "young deer, gazelle". A biblical name; borne by several male figures. The name is now used as both a boy's name, and as a girl's name.

Oracia
Pronunciation: OR-a-cee-a
Oracia is of Spanish origin. The meaning of the name Oracia is unknown. The name is a feminine form of the Latin clan name, Horace.

Oralee
Pronunciation: OR-a-lee
The name Oralee is of Hebrew origin. The meaning of Oralee is "my light". Oralee is a variant of the English name Auralee.

Oriana
Pronunciation: or-ee-AHN-ah
The name Oriana is of Latin origin. The meaning of Oriana is "Sunrise". From Latin oriri. The name first appeared in the 14th-century romance, Amadis de Gaul.

Orla
Pronunciation: OR-lah
The name Orla is of Irish, Gaelic, and Celtic origin. The meaning of Orla is "Princess".

P

Paloma

Pronunciation: pa-LOH-mah

Paloma is of Latin origin. The meaning of the name Paloma is "dove". Paloma is a Spanish name.

Pamela

Pronunciation: PAM-eh-lah

The name Pamela was invented by the poet Sir Philip Sidney (1554-86). He used the name for his heroine in his book, Arcadia (1590). Samuel Richardson popularised the name with his novel, Pamela (1740).

Pandora

Pronunciation: pan-DOE-ah

Pandora is of Greek origin. The meaning of the name Pandora is "all gifts". Borne in Greek mythology; Pandora was the beautiful, but foolish first mortal, created by the Greek god of fire to avenge the theft of fire by Prometheus. Pandora was given charge of a mysterious box and told never to open it up. However, Pandora could not resist opening the box, and in doing so she released all of the humankind's ills into the world, followed by one counterpart, Hope.

Paris

Pronunciation: PARE-iss

The name Paris is of Greek origin. In Greek mythology, Paris was the name of the young prince of Troy, whose love affair with Helen caused the Trojan war. Paris is used as both a boy's name, and as a girl's name. The name was also an English given surname for immigrants from the capital of France.

Pascale

Pronunciation: PAS-cale

The name Pascale is of French and Hebrew origin. The meaning of Pascale is "pertaining to Easter". Pascale is the feminine form of the French name Pascal. Early Christians often gave the name to children born at Passover.

Patience

Pronunciation: PAY-shuns

The name Patience is of English origin. The meaning of the name Patience is "enduring, forbearing". Patience is one of the several abstract nouns denoting admirable qualities. The name was popular among Puritans in the 16th century.

Patricia

Pronunciation: pa-TRISH-ah

The name Patricia is of Latin origin. The meaning of Patricia is "noble". Patricia is a feminine form derived from patricius, which means 'nobleman.' The name is also a feminine form of Patrick. Diminutives: Pat, Patsy, Pattie, Patty, Tricia, Trish.

Patsy

Pronunciation: PAT-see

The name Patsy is of Latin origin. The meaning of Patsy is "noble, patrician". Patsy is a diminutive of the name Patricia.

Paula

Pronunciation: PAW-lah

The name Paula is of Latin origin. The meaning of Paula is "small". Paula is a feminine form of the masculine name Paul. A 4th-century Saint Paula founded a number of convents in and around Bethlehem.

Paulette
Pronunciation: PAWL-ette
The name Paulette is of Latin origin. The meaning of Paulette is "small". Paulette is a French diminutive form of the Latin name Paula.

Paulina
Pronunciation: pawl-EEN-ah
The name Pauline is of Latin origin. The meaning of Paulina is "small". Paulina is a Latinate diminutive form of the name Paula.

Pauline
Pronunciation: pawl-EEN
The name Pauline is of Latin origin. The meaning of Pauline is "small". The name is a French form of Paulina.

Penelope
Pronunciation: pen-NELL-a-pee
Penelope is of Greek origin. The meaning of the name Penelope is "weaver". Borne in Greek mythology; Penelope was the wife of Odysseus. She passed his ten-year absence in spinning, loyally fending off all suitors. She was the model of domestic virtues. The name has come to signify a loyal, and intelligent woman. Diminutives: Pen, Penny.

Pepita
Pronunciation: p(e)-pi-ta
The name Pepita is of Spanish origin. The meaning of Pepita is "Jehovah increases". Pepita is a feminine form of Joseph.

Peta
Pronunciation: PET-ah
The name Peta is of Spanish and Greek origin. The meaning of Peta is "rock". Peta is a variant of the Spanish name Papita. The name is also a variant of the Greek name Petra. Peta is a modern feminine form of the masculine name Peter.

Petra
Pronunciation: PEH-trah
The name Petra is of Greek origin. The meaning of Petra is "rock". Petra is a feminine form of the masculine name Peter, derived from Greek petra.

Petrova
Pronunciation: PET-rova
The name Petrova is of Greek and Russian origin. The meaning Petrova is "rock". Petrova is a Russian feminine form of the name Peter.

Petula
Pronunciation: pe-tu-LAH
Petula is of Latin origin. The meaning of the name Petula is "to ask, to seek". Possibly derived from the Latin petulare.

Philippa
Pronunciation: FIL-lip-ah
The name Philippa is of Greek origin. The meaning of Philippa is "horse lover". Philippa is a feminine form of the

masculine name Philip. Diminutives: Phil, Phillie, Philly, Pip, Pippa, Pippi, Pippy.

Philomena
Pronunciation: pa-LOH-mah
Philomena is of Greek origin. The meaning of Philomena is "beloved". The name was borne by two early Roman saints. Diminutives: Mena, Mina, Phil, Phillie, Philly.

Phoebe
Pronunciation: FEE-bee
Phoebe is of Greek origin. The meaning of the name Phoebe is "bright, radiant". Borne in Greek mythology; it was the title given to the Greek goddess of the moon, Artemis. The name became popular in the 18th century.

Pia
Pronunciation: PEE-ah
The name Pia is of Latin origin. The meaning of Pia is "pious". The name is a feminine form of the Latin adjective pius.

Pilar
Pronunciation: pee-LAR
The name Pilar is of Spanish origin. The meaning of Pilar is "pillar". From Nuestra Señora del Pilar, which means, 'Our Lady of the Pillar'. In the Catholic tradition, it is a reference to a legendary appearance of the Virgin Mary standing on a pillar at Saragossa.

Pippa
Pronunciation: PIPP-a
Pippa is of Greek origin. The meaning of the name Pippa is "lover of horses". Pippa is a diminutive of the Greek name Phillipa.

Polly
Pronunciation: PAH-lee
The name Polly is of English and Irish origin. The meaning of Polly is "star of the sea". Polly is a variant of the name Molly, which is a nickname for Mary.

Pollyanna
Pronunciation: POLL-ee-ann-a
The name Pollyanna was invented by Eleanor Porter for the heroine in her children's book, Pollyanna (1913).

Poppy
Pronunciation: POP-ee
The name Poppy is of Latin origin. The meaning of Poppy is unknown. From Latin papaver, donating a species of flower that has papery leaves.

Posy
Pronunciation: POH-see
The name Posy is of English origin. The meaning of Posy is "a bunch of flowers". Posy is also used as a nickname for Josephine.

Primrose
Pronunciation: PRIM-rose
The name Primrose is of Latin origin. The meaning of Primrose is "first rose". From Latin prima rosa. Primrose is also a botanical name of a 19th-century yellow

flower which blooms early in spring, particularly on banks and in woodlands.

Princess
Pronunciation: PRIN-sess
The name Princess if of English origin. Princess is a title name used by Royalty.

Priscilla
Pronunciation: pris-SILL-ah
Priscilla is of Latin origin. The meaning of the name Priscilla is "ancient". Priscilla is a feminine diminutive of the Roman family name Priscus. A biblical name: Priscilla was a first-century Christian missionary. The name was adopted by the Puritans.
Diminutives: Cilla, Pris.

Prudence
Pronunciation: PROO-dens
The name Prudence is of Latin origin. The meaning of Prudence is "caution, discretion". The name was popular during the 16th, 17th and 19th centuries.

Prunella
Pronunciation: PRU-nell-a
The name Prunella is of Latin origin. The meaning of Prunella is "small plum".

Psyche
Pronunciation: p-sy-che
The name Psyche is of Greek origin. The meaning of Psyche is "breath, of the soul". Borne in mythology; Psyche was a mortal girl who fell in love with Cupid.

Purity
Pronunciation: PUR-it-ee
The name Purity if of Middle English origin. Purity is a virtue name.

Q

Qiturah
Pronunciation: KWIT-ur-ah
The name Qiturah is of Arabic origin. The meaning of Qiturah is "incense, scent".

Queenie
Pronunciation: KWE-nee
The name Queenie is of English origin. The meaning of Queenie is "Queen". From Old cwen, which means 'woman.' Queenie was a name used by contemporaries to refer to Queen Victoria. The name was popular during the 20th century.

Quenby
Pronunciation: KWIN-bee
The name Quenby is of Old English origin. The meaning of Quenby is "Queen's settlement". Quenby is also a place name.

Querida
Pronunciation: kare-EE-sah
The name Querida is of Spanish origin. The meaning of Querida is "beloved".

Questa
Pronunciation: KWES-ta
The name Questa is of French origin. The meaning of Questa is "one who seeks".

Quiana
Pronunciation: kee-AHN-ah
The name Quiana is of American origin. The meaning of Quiana is "silky". The name is also possibly a variant of the name Hannah or Ayana.

Queta
Pronunciation: KAY-tah
The name Queta is of Spanish origin. The meaning of Queta is unknown.

Quilla
Pronunciation: KWIL-la
The name Quilla is of Middle English origin. The meaning of Quilla is "feather".

Quincey
Pronunciation: KWIN-cey
Quincey is of Old French origin. The meaning of the name Quincey is "estate of the fifth son". Adopted surname, originally a baronial name from Cuinchy in northern France. Quincey can be used as a both a girl's name, and as a boy's name.

Quinn
Pronunciation: KWIN
The name Quinn is of Irish and Gaelic origin. The meaning of Quinn is "counsel". An adopted Irish surname, from the Gaelic name O Cuinn, meaning 'decedent of Conn.' Quinn has been used a given name from very ancient times. Quinn is used as both a girl's name, and as a boy's name.

Quintina
Pronunciation: KWIN-te-na
Quintina is of Latin origin. The meaning of the name Quintina is "fifth".

Quirina
Pronunciation: KW-ree-na
The name Quirina is of Latin origin. The meaning of Quirina is "Warrior".

R

Rachana
Pronunciation: ra-SHA-nah
Rachana is of Hindi origin. The meaning of the name Rachana is "creation".

Rachel
Pronunciation: RAY-cehl
The name Rachel is of Hebrew origin. The meaning of Rachel is "ewe, female sheep". A biblical name; borne in the Old Testament by the wife of Jacob, and mother of Benjamin and Joseph. She was described as being 'beautiful in form and countenance'. She died while giving birth to Benjamin. The name was popularised in the hit TV series, Friends (1994-2004). Diminutives: Rach, Rae.

Radha
Pronunciation: RAD-ha
The name Radha is of Hindi and Sanskrit origin. The meaning of Radha is "success". In Hindu religion, Radha was the name of a cowherd who became the favourite consort of Krishna.

Rae
Pronunciation: ray
The name Rae is of Hebrew origin. The meaning of Rae is "ewe, female sheep". Rae is a diminutive of the name Rachel.

Rafaela
Pronunciation: rah-fah-AY-lah
The name Rafaela is of Spanish origin. The meaning of Rafaela is "God has healed". Rafaela is a feminine form of the masculine name Raphael.

Raphaela
Pronunciation: rah-fah-AY-lah
The name Raphaela is of Spanish origin. The meaning of Raphaela is "God has healed". Raphaela is a feminine form of the masculine name Raphael.

Ramona
Pronunciation: ra-MOH-nah
The name Ramona is of Spanish and Old German origin. The meaning of Ramona is "protecting hands". Ramona is a feminine form of the masculine name Roman, the Spanish form of Raymond.

Raquel
Pronunciation: rah-KELL
Raquel is of Spanish and Portuguese origin. The meaning of the name Raquel is "ewe, female sheep". Raquel is a Spanish form of the name Rachel.

Rebecca
Pronunciation: ree-BEK-ah
The name Rebecca is of Hebrew origin. The meaning of Rebecca is "to bind". Rebecca is a Latin form of the Hebrew name Rebekah. The name was popularised in the 20th century, possibly due to Daphne du Maurier's novel Rebecca (1938). The novel was later made into a film by Alfred Hitchcock in 1940. Diminutives: Becca, Becky.

Regan
Pronunciation: REE-gan
Regan is of Gaelic origin. The meaning of the name Regan is unknown. Shakespeare

used the name for one of the king's three daughters in King Lear (1606).

Renata
Pronunciation: REN-at-ah
The name Renata is of Latin origin. The meaning of Renata is "Reborn". Renata is a Latinate form of the name Renèe. The name was adopted by the Puritans.

Rene, Renie
Pronunciation: REN-ee
The name Rene is of Greek origin. The meaning of Rene is "peace". Rene is a diminutive of the Greek name Irene.

Rhiannon
Pronunciation: ree-ANN-on
The name Rhiannon is of Welsh origin. The meaning of Rhiannon is "goddess, great queen". Borne in mythology; by a figure in the Mabinogian, the collection of Welsh legends.

Rhoda
Pronunciation: ROH-da
The name Rhoda is of Greek and Latin origin. The meaning of Rhoda is "rose". From Greek rhodon. A biblical name; borne by a servant girl who was one of the early Christian disciples. The name was popular during the 18th and 19th centuries.

Rhona
Pronunciation: ROH-nah
Rhona is of uncertain origin. Rhona is a feminine form of the masculine name Ronald.

Rica
Pronunciation: REE-kah
The name Rica is of Old Norse origin. The meaning of Rica is "complete ruler". Rica is a diminutive of any girl's name ending – rica, such as Erica or Frederica.

Rika
Pronunciation: re-KAH
The name Rika is of Old Norse origin. The meaning of Rika is "complete ruler". Rika is a diminutive of any girl's name ending – rica, such as Erica or Frederica.

Rita
Pronunciation: REE-tah
The name Rita is of Spanish origin. The name is originally a diminutive of Margarita, the Spanish form of Margaret. The Italian Saint Rita is regarded as the patron saint of unhappy marriages and desperate cases.

Roberta
Pronunciation: roh-BER-tah
The name Roberta is of Old English and Old German origin. The meaning of Roberta is "bright, fame". Roberta is a feminine form of the masculine name Robert. Diminutives: Bobbie, Bobby.

Robin
Pronunciation: RAH-bin
Robin is of English origin. The meaning of the name Robin is unknown. The name is a 20th-century adoption of a well establish boy's name for girls. Robyn has also been

used as a nickname for males named Robert. Robyn is also the name of a red-breasted songbird.

Róisín
Pronunciation: ROE-sheen
The name Róisín is of Irish Gaelic origin. The meaning of Róisín is "little rose".

Romaine
Pronunciation: ROE-may-ne
The name Romaine is of French origin. The meaning of Romaine is "Woman of Rome".

Ros
Pronunciation: ros
The name Ros is of Old German origin. The meaning of Ros is "gentle horse, horse protector". Ros is a diminutive of Rosalind, Rosamund or any name beginning with Ros-.

Rosa
Pronunciation: ROH-za
Rosa is of Latin origin. The meaning of the name Rosa is "rose". Rosa is a Latinate form of Rose.

Rosalie
Pronunciation: ROH-za-lee
The name Rosalie is of French origin. The meaning of Rosalie is "rose garden". Rosalie is a French name derived from the Latin name Rosa. Saint Rosalie was a 12th-century virgin martyr of Palermo, Sicily.

Rosalind
Pronunciation: RAH-za-lind
The name Rosalind is of Old German origin. The meaning of Rosalind is "gentle horse". Shakespeare popularised the name in As You Like It (1603). Rosalind was the name of the heroine. Diminutives: Ros, Roz.

Rosaline
Pronunciation: ROZ-a-lin
The name Rosaline is of French origin. The meaning of Rosaline is "gentle horse". Rosaline is a variation of the name Rosalind.

Rosamond
Pronunciation: ROH-za-mond
The name Rosamond is of Old German origin. The meaning of Rosamond is "horse protector". The name dates back to the Middle Ages.

Rosamund
Pronunciation: ROH-za-mund
The name Rosamund is of French origin. The meaning of Rosamund is "horse protector". The name was associated with the Latin rosa mundi, which means, 'rose of the world.' An epithet that was given to the Virgin Mary. Diminutives: Ros, Rosa, Roz.

Rosanna
Pronunciation: ROSE-an-ah
The name Rosanna is an 18th-century coinage combining the names Rose and Anna together.

Rosanne
Pronunciation: ROSE-anne

The name Rosanne is a 19th-century coinage combining the names Rose and Anne together.

Rose

Pronunciation: rohz

The name Rose is of Latin origin. The meaning of Rose is "rose". Rose is derived from Latin, rosa. The name denotes a shrub of the genus rosa, fragrant flowers with thorny stems. The name was introduced to Britain by the Normans in the 11th century. Diminutives: Rosie.

Rosemary

Pronunciation: ROHZ-mare-ee

The name Rosemary is of Latin origin. The meaning of Rosemary is "dew of the sea". Rosemary is also the name of a fragrant herb. Diminutives: Romey, Romy.

Rosetta

Pronunciation: ROE-set-ah

Rosetta is of Latin origin. The meaning of the name Rosetta is "rose". Rosetta is a variation of the name Rose. Originally an Italian diminutive, that dates back to the 19th century.

Rosheen

Pronunciation: ROE-she-n

The name Rosheen is of Irish Gaelic origin. The meaning of Rosheen is "little rose". Rosheen is an Anglicisation of the Irish Gaelic name Roísín.

Rosie

Pronunciation: ROSE-ee

The name Rosie is of Latin origin. The meaning of the name Rosie is "rose". Rosie is a diminutive of all names that contain the element, 'Rose'.

Rosina

Pronunciation: ROS-in-ah

The name Rosina is of Latin origin. The meaning of Rosina is "rose". Originally a Spanish diminutive, Rosina is a variation of the name Rose.

Rowan

Pronunciation: ROH-an

The name Rowan is of Gaelic origin. The meaning of Rowan is "red berry tree". Rowan is used as both a girl's name and as a boy's name.

Rowena

Pronunciation: roh-EEN-ah

The name Rowena is of Old German origin. The meaning of Rowena is "fame and happiness". Rowena is also possibly a variation of the Welsh name Rhonwen.

Roxanne

Pronunciation: roks-ANN

Roxanne is of Persian origin. The meaning of the name Roxanne is "Dawn". The name is borne by a Persian wife of Alexander the Great. Diminutive: Roxy.

Ruby

Pronunciation: ROO-bee

The name Ruby is of English origin. The meaning of Ruby is "the red gemstone". From Latin rubus. Ruby is the name of a precious red stone, considered by the Ancients to be an antidote to poison and protection from the plague. Some people consider Rubies to be bad luck. Rubies are the birthstone of July.

Ruth

Pronunciation: rooth

The name Ruth is of Hebrew origin. The meaning of Ruth is "friend". A biblical name; borne in the Old Testament by the loyal wife of Boaz. Ruth was the young Moabite widow and daughter-in-law of Naomi. The name was popular during the 17th century. Diminutives: Ruthi, Ruthie.

S

Sabrina

Pronunciation: sa-BREE-nah

Sabrina is of Celtic origin. The meaning of Sabrina is unknown. Sabrina is a Roman name for the River Severn. Borne in mythology; the name of the illegitimate daughter of King Locrine of Wales. She was drowned in the River Severn by her father's ex-wife, Gwendolen. The Old Man of the Sea took pity on her and turned her into a river goddess.

Sadie

Pronunciation: SAY-dee

The name Sadie is of Hebrew origin. The meaning of Sadie is "Princess". Sadie is a diminutive for the names, Sarah and Mercedes. The name was first used as a first name at the beginning of the 20th century.

Saffron

Pronunciation: SAFF-ron

Saffron is of Arabic origin. Derived from Arabic zafaran. Saffron is the most expensive of all spices. Saffron is also a bright orange/yellow colour dye.

Sally

Pronunciation: SAL-ee

The name Sally is of Hebrew origin. The meaning of Sally is "Princess". Sally is a diminutive of Sarah, often used in its own right. The name was popular in the 18th and 20th centuries. Diminutives: Sal.

Samantha

Pronunciation: sa-MAN-thah

The name Samantha is of English origin. The meaning of Samantha is "listen, God heard". American Actress, Elizabeth Montgomery popularised the name Samantha during the 1960's in the hit TV show, Bewitched.

Sanchia

Pronunciation: san-CHIA

The name Sanchia is of Spanish origin. The meaning of Sanchia is "holy, sacred". Sanchia is a variant of the Latin name Sancia. The name was introduced into Britain during the 13th century.

Sandie, Sandy

Pronunciation: SAN-dee

Sandy is of uncertain origin. The meaning of the name Sandy is "man's defender". Diminutives of Alexandra, Cassandra, and Sandra.

Sandra

Pronunciation: SAN-drah

The name Sandra is of English origin. The meaning of Sandra is "man's defender". Sandra is a variation of the name Alexandra, via the Italian form, Alessandra.

Saorise

Pronunciation: seer-sha

The name Saorise is of Irish Gaelic origin. The meaning of Saorise is "freedom".

Sapphire

Pronunciation: SAFF-ire

The name Sapphire is of English origin. From Old French safir, derived from Greek sappheiros. Sapphire is a jewel name and the birthstone for September. A Sapphire is a transparent blue precious stone.

Sara, Sarah
Pronunciation: SARE-ah
The name Sarah is of Hebrew origin. The meaning of Sarah is "Princess". A biblical name; borne by the wife of Abraham and mother of Isaac, whom she conceived when she was 90 years old. Originally called Sarai, she was given the name Sarah at God's command. Sarah lived an adventurous and nomadic life. She was described as being exceptionally beautiful. The name became popular in the 16th century.

Sarina
Pronunciation: sa-REE-nah
The name Sarina is of Latin origin. The meaning of Sarina is "Princess". Sarina is a variant of the Hebrew name Sarah.

Sarita
Pronunciation: sa-RE-ta
The name Sarita is of Hebrew origin. The meaning of Sarita is "Princess". Sarita is a variant of the Hebrew name Sarah.

Sasha
Pronunciation: SAH-shah
Sasha is of Greek and Russian origin. The meaning of the name Sasha is "man's defender". Sasha is a Russian diminutive of the name Alexandra. Sasha is used as both a girl's name, and as a boy's name.

Saskia
Pronunciation: SAS-kee-a
Saskia is of Danish and Old German origin. The meaning of the name Saskia is "the Saxon people". Saskia was the name of the wife of the Dutch painter, Rembrandt (17th century).

Scarlett
Pronunciation: SCAR-let
The name Scarlett is of Old French origin. The meaning of Scarlett is "red". An adopted surname derived originally from Old French escarlate, which means 'scarlet cloth.' Margaret Mitchell popularised the name in her epic novel, Gone With The Wind (1936). Scarlett O' Hara was the name of the heroine.

Selena, Selina
Pronunciation: sa-LEEN-ah
The name Selina is of uncertain origin. The meaning of Selina is "the moon". The name was first used in Britain during the Middles Ages.

Selma
Pronunciation: SEL-mah
The name Selma is of Old German and Arabic origin. The meaning of Selma is "safe, peace".

Serena
Pronunciation: ser-REE-nah
Serena is of Latin origin. The meaning of the name Serena is "calm, serene". From Latin serenus, meaning 'calm.' Borne by a Christian saint.

Shannon
Pronunciation: SHAN-en

Shannon is of Gaelic origin. The meaning of the name Shannon is "old". Originally an adopted surname, derived from Ireland's principal river.

Sharon

Pronunciation: SHARE-en

The name Sharon is of Hebrew origin. The meaning of Sharon is "a fertile plain". A biblical place name, from the plain of Sharon in the Holy Land. The name was adopted by the Puritans.

Sheba

Pronunciation: SHEE-bah

The name Sheba is of Hebrew origin. The meaning of Sheba is "promise". Sheba is a diminutive of Bathsheba, which is associated with the Queen of Sheba. She visited Solomon in search of information about his God. Balkis, Queen of Sheba, also appears in the Koran. Sheba is the name of a kingdom in southern Arabia noted for its great wealth.

Sheila

Pronunciation: SHEE-lah

The name Sheila is of Irish and Gaelic origin. The meaning of the name Sheila is "blind". Sheila is an anglicised form of the Irish Gaelic name, Síle.

Shelley

Pronunciation: SHEL-ee

The name Shelley is of Old English origin. The meaning of Shelley is "sloped meadow". An adopted surname and place name from Old English, meaning 'wood on a slope.' Shelley is also used a nickname for Michelle, Rochelle, and Shirley. Shelley is used as both a girl's name, and as a boy's name.

Sheridan

Pronunciation: SHARE-a-den

The name Sheridan is of Irish and Gaelic origin. The meaning of Sheridan is "seeker". An adopted Irish surname, from O Sirideain. The name was popularised by Irish playwright Richard Brinsley Sheridan (1751-1861). The name is used as both a boy's name and, as a girl's name.

Sherry

Pronunciation: SHARE-ee

The name Sherry is of English origin. The meaning of Sherry is "darling, dear". From French chèrie. The name is also a short form of the Hebrew name Sharon.

Shona

Pronunciation: SH-o-na

The name Shona is of Gaelic and Hebrew origin. The meaning of Shona is "God is gracious". Shona is a Gaelic feminine form of the name John.

Sian

Pronunciation: shaahn

The name Sian is of Welsh origin. The meaning of Sian is "God's grace". Sian is a Welsh variant of the name Jane.

Siena

Pronunciation: see-EN-ah

Siena is of Latin origin. The meaning of the name Siena is "from Siena". Originally a place name of the city, Siena in Italy. Siena is also the name of a reddish shade of brown.

Sidney, Sydney

Pronunciation: SID-nee

Sidney is of Old English origin. The meaning of the name Sidney is "wide meadow". Sidney is an adopted surname and place name. The name has been used as a first name since the 17th century. Charles Dickens boosted the popularity of the name when he used it for his hero in A Tale Of Two Cities (1859). The Australian city of Sydney was named in honour of Thomas Townshend. The name is used as both a boy's name, and as a girl's name.

Silvia

Pronunciation: SIL-vee-ah

The name Silvia is of Latin origin. The meaning of Silvia is "wood, forest". From the Latin name Silvius. Shakespeare used the name in The Two Gentlemen of Verona (1594).

Simone

Pronunciation: sih-MOHN

The name Simone is of Hebrew origin. The meaning of Simone is "hear, listen". Simone is a feminine form of the masculine name Simon. Simone is used as both a girl's name, and as a boy's name.

Sinèad

Pronunciation: sha-NADE

The name Sinèad is of Irish Gaelic origin. The meaning of Sinèad is "God is gracious". Sinèad is an Irish Gaelic form of the name Janet.

Siobhan

Pronunciation: sha-VAHN

The name Siobhan is of Irish Gaelic and Hebrew origin. The meaning of Siobhan is "God is gracious". Siobhan is an Irish Gaelic form of the name Joan.

Sky, Skye

Pronunciation: sky

The name Sky is of English origin. Sky is one of several nature names that became popular when nature names were made fashionable during 1960's. Skye is associated with the Isle of Skye in Scotland. Sky is used as both a girl's name, and as a boy's name.

Skyler

Pronunciation: SKY-ler

Skyler is of Dutch origin. The meaning of the name Skyler is "fugitive".

Sonia

Pronunciation: SOHN-yah

The name Sonia is of Greek origin. The meaning of Sonia is "wisdom". Sonia is a Russian variation of the name Sophia. Stephen McKenna popularised the name with his novel, Sonia (1917).

Sonja

Pronunciation: SON-ja

The name Sonja is of Greek origin. The meaning of Sonja is "wisdom". Sonja is a Russian variation of the name Sophia.

Sophia
Pronunciation: so-FEE-ah
Sophia is of Greek origin. The meaning of the name Sophia is "wisdom". The name was introduced to Britain in the 17th century by the granddaughter of James I.

Sophie
Pronunciation: so-FEE
Sophie is of French origin. The meaning of the name Sophie is "wisdom". The name was introduced to Britain in the 17th century by the granddaughter of James I.

Sorcha
Pronunciation: SAW-kha
The name Sorcha is of Irish and Gaelic origin. The meaning of Sorcha is "bright".

Sorrel
Pronunciation: s(or)-rell
The name Sorrel is of Old French and Old German origin. The meaning of Sorrel is "sour". From the Old French plant name, surele, derived from sur, which means 'sour.' This refers to the acid taste of its leaves.

Stacey, Stacie, Stacy
Pronunciation: ST-aa-cee
The name Stacey is of Greek origin. The meaning of Stacey is "Resurrection". Stacey is a diminutive of the Greek name Anastasia, and of the name Eustacia.

Stella
Pronunciation: STELL-ah
The name Stella is of Latin origin. The meaning of the name Stella is "star".

Stephanie
Pronunciation: STEFF-a-nee
The name Stephanie is of Greek origin. The meaning of Stephanie is "garland, crown". Stephanie is a feminine form of the masculine name Stephan. Diminutives: Steff, Steffi, Steffie, Steph, Stephie.

Stevie
Pronunciation: STE-vie
The name Stevie is of Greek origin. The meaning of Stevie is "garland, crown". The name is originally a diminutive of Stephen. The name is used as both a girl's name, and as a boy's name.

Summer
Pronunciation: SUH-mer
The name Summer is of Old English origin. Summer is one of several names derived from nature. The name was popularised during the 1960's when nature names became fashionable.

Susanna, Susannah, Suzanna
Pronunciation: SU-zan-ah
The name Suzanna is of Hebrew origin. The meaning of Suzanna is "lily". From the Hebrew name Shushannah.

T

Tabitha

Pronunciation: TAB-i-thah

The name Tabitha is of Aramaic origin. The meaning of Tabitha is "gazelle". A biblical name; borne by a New Testament figure, the Aramaic name of Dorcas. She was a kind woman noted for her good work, who was resurrected by St Peter.

Tacy

Pronunciation: TAY-cee

The name Tacy is of Latin origin. The meaning of Tacy is "silence". The name may be a short form of Anastasia.

Taffy

Pronunciation: TAFF-ee

The name Taffy is of Welsh origin. The meaning of Taffy is "loved one".

Tahira

Pronunciation: TA-hi-ra

Tahira is of Arabic origin. The meaning of the name Tahira is "virginal, pure".

Taima

Pronunciation: ta(i)-MAH

The name Taima is of Native American Indian origin. The meaning of Taima is "pearl of thunder".

Talia

Pronunciation: TAL-yah

The name Talia is of Hebrew and Aramaic origin. The meaning of Talia is "heaven's dew". The name is a variant of Taliah. Talia is also a short form of the name Natalia.

Tallulah

Pronunciation: TAL-oo-lah

The name Tallulah is of Native American Indian origin. The meaning of Tallulah is "running water, leaping water". The Choctaws lived near the Tallulah waterfall.

Tamara

Pronunciation: TAM-a-rah

Tamara is of Hebrew origin. The meaning of the name Tamara is "date palm". The name is a Russian variant of Tamar, borne by a 12th-century Queen of Georgia. Diminutives: Tammie, Tammy.

Tamsin

Pronunciation: TAM-sin

The name Tamsin is of English origin. The meaning of Tamsin is unknown. Tamsin is a short form of the Aramaic name Thomasina, the feminine form of Thomas. The name dates back to the Middle Ages.

Tania, Tanya

Pronunciation: THAN-ya

The name Tania is of Russian origin. The meaning of Tania is unknown. Tania is a Russian diminutive of Tatiana.

Tansy

Pronunciation: TAN-see

The name Tansy is of Greek origin. The meaning of Tansy is "eternal life". From old French tanesie, derived from Greek anthanasi, which means 'immortal.' Tansy is also the name of a bitter tasting, aromatic herb. The name was adopted as a first name in the 1960's.

Tara

Pronunciation: TAH-rah

Tara is of Gaelic and Sanskrit origin. The meaning of the name Tara is "hill, star". Ancient Tara is the name of a place in County Meath, 'stone of destiny' where Irish kings resided. The name was popularised by the Hollywood film, Gone with the Wind (1939). Tara is the name of Scarlett O'Hara's family estate. Borne in Hindu mythology; Tara is one of the names of the wife of Shiva. In Mahayana Buddhism, Tara is the name of the wife of Buddha.

Tatiana

Pronunciation: tat-YAH-nah

Tatiana is of Latin and Russian origin. The meaning of the name Tatiana is "of the family of Tatius". From the feminine form of the Latin name Tatianus. Tatiana is also the name of a 3rd-century saint.

Tegan

Pronunciation: TEA-gan

The name Tegan is of Welsh origin. The meaning of Tegan is "beautiful".

Teresa

Pronunciation: ter-REE-sah

The name Teresa is of Greek origin. The meaning of Teresa is "late summer". The first bearers of the name might have been from the Greek island of Therasia. The name is popular among Roman Catholic saints. Saint Thèrese of Lisieux (1873-97) was a young Carmelite nun who wrote her autobiography while she lay dying of tuberculosis. Mother Teresa founded an order of nuns, the Missionaries of Charity, whose sisters help people in need around the world. Mother Teresa's hard work earned her the title, 'the saint of the gutters'.

Theresa

Pronunciation: ter-REE-sah

The name Theresa is of Greek origin. The meaning of Theresa is "late summer". The first bearers of the name might possibly have been from the Greek island of Therasia. The name is popular among Roman Catholic saints.

Tess

Pronunciation: TESS

The name Tess is of Greek origin. The meaning of Tess is "late summer". Tess is diminutive of Teresa and Theresa; the name became popular in its own right. Tomas Hardy popularised the name with his famous novel, Tess of the d'Ubervilles (1891).

Tessa

Pronunciation: TESS-ah

Tessa is of English origin. The meaning of the name Tessa is "fourth child".
Tessa is diminutive of Teresa and Theresa; the name became popular in its own right.

Thea

Pronunciation: THEE-ah

Thea is of Greek origin. The meaning of the name Thea is "goddess". Thea is a short form of Althea, Mathea, and Dorothea.

Theodora
Pronunciation: thee-a-DOR-ah
The name Theodora is of Greek origin. The meaning of Theodora is "God's gift". Theodora is a feminine form of the masculine name Theodore.

Tiana
Pronunciation: tee-AHN-ah
Tiana is of Latin and Russian origin. The meaning of the name Tiana is 'of the family of Tatius'. Tiana is a diminutive of Tatiana.

Tiffany
Pronunciation: TIF-a-nee
The name Tiffany is of Greek origin. The meaning of Tiffany is "revelation of God.". Tiffany is a variant of the Greek name Theophania. The name refers to manifestations of God, particularly Epiphany. In many Christian countries, females who are born on 6th January (the Feast of Epiphany) are given some form of this name. The name was made popular by the New York jeweler, Tiffany & Co.

Tilda
Pronunciation: TIL-da
The name Tilda is of German origin. The meaning of Tilda is "mighty in battle". Tidla is a diminutive of the Old German name Matilda.

Tilly
Pronunciation: TILL-ee
The name Tilly is of German origin. The meaning of Tilly is "mighty in battle". Tilly is a diminutive of the Old German name Matilda. Tillly is also a variant of the name Tilda.

Tina
Pronunciation: TEE-nah
The name Tina is of Latin origin. The meaning of the name Tina is "follower of Christ". Originally a diminutive for Christiana, the name is now used in its own right.

Toni
Pronunciation: TOH-nee
The name Toni is of English origin. The meaning of Toni is unknown. Toni is a diminutive of Antonia, Antonina, and Antoinette.

Tonia, Tonya
Pronunciation: TOHN-yah
The name Tonia is of French origin. The meaning of Tonia is unknown. Tonia is French feminine diminutive of the name Antoine.

Tracie, Tracy, Tracey
Pronunciation: T-race-ee
The name Tracie is of Greek origin. The meaning of Tracie is "late summer". Variations of Teresa. The name was popularised by the character of Tracey Lord in the film The Philadelphia Story (1940).

Trina
Pronunciation: TREEN-nah

Trina is of Scandinavian origin. The meaning of the name Trina is "pure". Trina is diminutive for the Greek name Katrina.

Trinity
Pronunciation: TRIN-ee-tee
The name Trinity is of Latin origin. The meaning of Trinity is "triad". The name refers to the Holy Trinity in Christian faith.

Trista
Pronunciation: TRISS-tah
Trista is of English origin. The meaning of the name Trista is "tryst". Trista is a feminine form of the masculine name Tristan.

Tristana
Pronunciation: TRIST-an-ah
The name Tristana is of Welsh origin. The meaning of Tristana is "tryst". Tristana is a feminine form of the masculine name Tristan.

Trixie
Pronunciation: TRIKS-ee
The name Trixie is of English origin. The meaning of Trixie is "blessed, voyager". Trixie is a diminutive of Beatrix.

Troy
Pronunciation: TR-oy
The name Troy is of Irish and Gaelic origin. The meaning of Troy is "descendant of the footsoldier". An adopted surname that was given to those who migrated to England from Troyes in France, after the Norman conquest of 1066. Troy is also associated with the ancient city in Asia Minor where the Trojan wars were fought. The name is used as both a boy's name, and as a girl's name.

Trudi, Trudie, Trudy
Pronunciation: TROO-dee
The name Trudi of Old German origin. The meaning of the name Trudi is "strength, strong spear". The name is frequently used as a nickname for people called Gertrude, Hiltrud, and Ermintrude.

Tryphena
Pronunciation: T-ryphe-na
The name Tryphena is of Greek origin. The meaning of Tryphena is "delicacy". A biblical name; Tryphena appears in one of Paul's epistles to the Romans.

Tuesday
Pronunciation: TUES-day
The name Tuesday is of Old English origin derived from the Old English, 'Tiwesdaeg', meaning 'Tiw's Day'. Tuesday is a day of the week.

Tulia
Pronunciation: TU-lee-a
Tulia is of Spanish and Latin origin. The meaning of the name Tulia is unknown. Derived from an ancient Roman family name, Tullius.

Tyler
Pronunciation: TYE-ler
The name Tyler is of English origin. The meaning of Tyler is "a worker in roof tiles".

Originally an occupational name. Tyler is used as both a girl's name and as a boy's name.

Tyra
Pronunciation: TEER-ah
The name Tyra is of Old English origin.
The meaning of Tyra is "Thor's battle".
The name was made famous by supermodel Tyra Banks.

U

Uberta
Pronunciation: OO-ber-TA
The name Uberta is of Italian origin. The meaning of Uberta is "shining intellect". Uberta is a variant of the Old German name Huberta.

Udele
Pronunciation: OO-del-e
The name Udele is of Old English origin. The meaning of the name Udele is "wealthy".

Ula
Pronunciation: oo-LA
Ula is of Celtic and Hawaiian origin. The meaning of the name Ula is "gem of the sea, wealthy".

Ulani
Pronunciation: uwl-an-EE
The name Ulani is of Hawaiian origin. The meaning of the name Ulani is "cheerful".

Ulima
Pronunciation: uwl-li-MA
The name Ulima is of Arabic origin. The meaning of the name Ulima is "wise".

Ulla
Pronunciation: uwl-LA
The name Ulla is of Old Norse origin. The meaning of Ulla is "will, determination".

Ulrica
Pronunciation: uwl-REE-kah
The name Ulrica is of Old German origin. The meaning of Ulrica is "power of the wolf". The name is a feminine form of Ulric.

Ultima
Pronunciation: uwl-ti-MA
The name Ultima is of Latin origin. The meaning of Ultima is "farthest point".

Ulva
Pronunciation: uwl-VA
The name Ulva is of Old German origin. The meaning of Ulva is "Wolf".

Ulyssa
Pronunciation: yoo-LISS-ah
The name Ulyssa is of Latin origin. The meaning of Ulyssa is unknown. The name is a feminine form of the masculine name Ulysses.

Uma
Pronunciation: OO-mah
The name Uma is of Hindi and Sanskrit origin. The meaning of Uma is "flax, turmeric". Borne by the goddess what mediates between Brahma and the other gods. Uma is also a byname for the Indian goddess Sakti, wife of Shiva. The Hebrew meaning of the name Uma is "nation".

Una
Pronunciation: OO-nah
Una is of Latin origin. The meaning of Una is "one". Anglicised form of the Irish Gaelic name, Ũna. The name was borne in Irish legend by the mother of Conn Cètchathach.

Udine
Pronunciation: un-DEE-ne

The name Udine if of Latin origin. The meaning of Udine is "little wave". Borne in mythology, Udine is the name of the spirit of the waters.

Unique

Pronunciation: yoo-NEEK

Unique is of Latin origin. The meaning of the name Unique is "only one".

Unity

Pronunciation: yoo-ni-TEE

The name Unity is of Middle English origin. The meaning of Unity is "oneness". The name was used by the Puritans.

Urania

Pronunciation: yoo-ran-IA

The name Urania is of Greek origin. The meaning of Urania is "heavenly". Borne in Greek mythology; Urania was the eldest of Zeus' and Mnemosyne's nine daughters. Zeus and Mnemosyne slept together for nine consecutive nights and birthed nine Muses; Urania was one of them. Urania was in charge of astronomy; she is often associated with universal love and the Holy Spirit. Urania inherited Zeus' majesty and power, and the beauty and grace of her Mnemosyne.

Urbana

Pronunciation: ur-BAN-a

The name Urbana is of Latin origin. The meaning of Urbana is "of the city". The name is a feminine form of Urban.

Uriela

Pronunciation: YOO-rie-la

The name Uriela is of Hebrew origin. The meaning of Uriela is "God's light".

Urit

Pronunciation: YOO-rit

The name Urit is of Hebrew origin. The meaning of Urit is "brightness".

Ursula

Pronunciation: UR-soo-lah

The name Ursula is of Latin and Scandinavian origin. The meaning of Ursula is "little bear". Several legends claim that Saint Ursula was a 4th-century British princess who went on a pilgrimage to Rome with her maiden companions, they were all massacred by the Huns at Cologne. Disney made the name famous in the film, The Little Mermaid (1989). Ursula is the name of the evil octopus.

Usha

Pronunciation: oo-shah

The name Usha is of Hindi and Sanskrit origin. The meaning of Usha is "Dawn". Borne in mythology, Usha was the daughter of heaven and the sister of night.

V

Val
Pronunciation: VAL
The name Val is a diminutive of Valda, Valentina, Valerie, or Valma.

Valda
Pronunciation: VAL-da
The name Valda is of Old German origin. The meaning of Valda is "renowned ruler". Valda is a feminine form of the name Waldemar.

Valen
Pronunciation: VA-len
Valen is a variant of the Latin name, Valentine. The meaning of the name Valen is "strong", "healthy". Valen is used as a both a boy's name, and as a girl's name.

Valencia
Pronunciation: vah-LEN-cee-ah
The name Valencia is of Latin origin. The meaning of Valencia is "strong". The name is a feminine form of Valentinus.

Valentina
Pronunciation: val-en-TEE-nah
The name Valentina is of Latin origin. The meaning of Valentina is "strong". The name is a feminine form of Valentine.

Valeria
Pronunciation: val-ER-e-a
Valeria is of Latin origin. The meaning of the name Valeria is "to be healthy". Valeria is a variant of the Latin name Valerie.

Valerie
Pronunciation: VAL-er-ee
The name Valerie is of Latin origin. The meaning of Valerie is "strong, healthy". The name is a French form of the Latin name, Valeria. Valerie is a feminine form of Valerius, a Roman family clan name. The name was borne by a 3rd-century saint.

Valeska
Pronunciation: VAL-esk-a
The name Valeska is of Slavic origin. The meaning of Valeska is "splendid leader". The name is a feminine form of Vladislav.

Valkyrie
Pronunciation: VALK-y-ree
The name Valkyrie is of Scandinavian origin. The meaning of Valkyrie is unknown. Borne in mythology; Valkyrie was an attendant of Odin.

Valley
Pronunciation: VAL-ee
The name Valley is a diminutive of Valerie. Valley is also a geography name, for a low spot in a landscape.

Vallombrosa
Pronunciation: VALL-om-bros-a
The name Vallombrosa is of Italian origin. The meaning of Vallombrosa is "shady valley". Vallombrosa is also a place name of a forest resort near Florence, Italy.

Valonia
Pronunciation: VAL-o-ne-a
The name Valonia is of Latin origin. The meaning of Valonia is "shallow valley". Valonia is also a place name.

Valora
Pronunciation: VAL-o-ra
The name Valora is of Latin origin. The meaning of Valora is "brave, courageous".

Vanda
Pronunciation: VAN-da
Vanda is of Italian and Czechoslovakian origin. The meaning of the name Vanda is "the tribe of Vandals". The name became popular in the 20th century.

Vanessa
Pronunciation: va-NESS-ah
The name Vanessa is of Greek origin. The meaning of Vanessa is "Butterfly". The name was invented by the author Jonathan Swift (1667-1745) for his friend Esther Vanhomrigh for Gulliver's Travels. He combined the first syllable of her Dutch surname name with Essa.

Vania
Pronunciation: VAHN-yah
Vania is of Latin origin. The meaning of the name Vania is "brings good news". The name is a variant of Ivana.

Vanita
Pronunciation: va-NEE-tah
The name Vanita is of Hindi origin. The meaning of Vanita is "woman".

Vanity
Pronunciation: VAN-ih-tee
The name Vanity is of French origin. The meaning of Vanity is "inflated in pride".

Vanna
Pronunciation: VAN-ah
The name Vanna is of Cambodian origin. The meaning of Vanna is "golden". Vanna is the feminine form of the name John.

Vanora
Pronunciation: VAHN-or-a
The name Vanora is of Old Welsh origin. The meaning of Vanora is "white wave".

Varda
Pronunciation: VAR-da
The name Varda is of Hebrew origin. The meaning of the name Varda is "rose".

Vashti
Pronunciation: VA-sh-tee
The name Vashti is of Persian origin. The meaning of Vashti is "beautiful". A biblical name; Vashti was the wife of King Ahasuerus of Persia. The king replaced his wife with Esther after she refused to display her beauty before his guests.

Vasilia
Pronunciation: VAS-il-a
The name Vasilia is of unknown origin. The meaning of Vasilia is "royal, kingly". Vasilia is a feminine form of the Greek name, Basil.

Veda
Pronunciation: VEE-da
Veda is of Sanskrit origin. The meaning of the name Veda is "knowledge". The Vedas are the four sacred books of the Hindus.

Vedette
Pronunciation: VEE-dett
The name Vedette is of Italian origin. The meaning of Vedette is "Sentry".

Vega
Pronunciation: VEE-ga
The name Vega is of Arabic origin. The meaning of Vega is "falling venture". Vega is also the name of the brightest star in the group of stars named, Lyra.

Velika
Pronunciation: VEL-ee-ka
The name Velika is of Slavic origin. The meaning of Velika is "great".

Velma
Pronunciation: VEL-ma
Velma is of English origin. The meaning of the name Velma is "determined protector". Velma is possibly a variant of the name Selma.

Velvet
Pronunciation: VEL-vet
The name Velvet is of English origin. The meaning of Velvet is unknown. Velvet is also the name of a soft fabric, which is associated with luxury.

Venerada
Pronunciation: VEN-er-ada
The name Venerada is of Spanish origin. The meaning of Venerada is "venerated".

Venetia
Pronunciation: ve-NEE-shah
The name Venetia is of Latin origin. The meaning of Venetia is "city of canals". From the Latin name for the city of Venice in Northern Italy. Venetia is also associated with the Roman goddess of love and fertility, Venus.

Venus
Pronunciation: VEE-nus
The name Venus is of Latin origin. The meaning of Venus is "love, fertility". Borne in Roman mythology; Venus is the Roman goddess of love and fertility.

Vera
Pronunciation: VEER-ah
Vera is of Russian and Slavic origin. The meaning of the name Vera is "faith". The name is often used as a nickname for Veronica and Guinevere.

Verbena
Pronunciation: VERB-en-a
The name Verbena is of Latin origin. The meaning of Verbena is "holy plants". The name was originally used to refer to the olive and myrtle plants, which had spiritual significance to the Romans.

Verena
Pronunciation: VER-ee-na
Verena is of Latin origin. The meaning of the name Verena is "true".

Verity
Pronunciation: VARE-i-tee

The name Verity is of Latin origin. The meaning of Verity is "truth". From the Latin word veritas. The name was adopted by the Puritans.

Verona
Pronunciation: VER-o-na
The name Verona is a short form of Veronica. The origin of the name is disputed. Verona is also the name of a northern Italian city.

Veronica
Pronunciation: ver-RON-ni-kah
Veronica is of Latin origin. The meaning of the name Veronica is "true image". From Latin vera icon. Saint Veronica was an Italian mystic. According to legend, St Veronica wiped the face of Jesus on his way to the cross. A 'true image' of Christ's face was left on the cloth. The name is a Latin form of the Greek name Berenice. The name was first used in Britain in the 17th century; the name was popular with Catholic families. Diminutives: Ronnie, Vero.

Veronique
Pronunciation: VER-on-i-k
The name Veronique is of French origin. The meaning of Veronique is "victory bringer". The name is a French form of Veronica.

Victoria
Pronunciation: vit-TOR-ee-ah
Victoria is of Latin origin. The meaning of the name Victoria is "victory". Victoria is a feminine form of Latin victorius. Borne in mythology; Victoria was a goddess who smiled on the people of ancient Rome for centuries. The name was adopted by early Christians. The name has been associated with Royalty after Queen Victoria (1819-1901) was given the name by her German mother. Diminutives: Vic, Vicki, Vickie, Vicky, Vikki, Vita, Tori, Toria, Tory.

Viola
Pronunciation: VI-o-la
The name Viola is of Latin origin. The meaning of Viola is "violet". Viola is a variant of the Latin name, Violet. The name was used by Shakespeare in Twelfth Night (1602).

Violet
Pronunciation: VYE-a-let
The name Violet is of Latin origin. The meaning of Violet is "purple". From Latin viola. Violet is the name of a low growing plant with purple or white flowers. The name became popular in the 19th century when flower names became fashionable.

Violetta
Pronunciation: VYE-el-et-a
The name Violetta is a variant of the Latin name, Violet. The meaning of Violetta is "purple".

Vivian
Pronunciation: VIV-ian
The name Vivian is of Latin origin. Old French form of the Latin name Vivianus, from vivus which means "alive," "lively."

The meaning of the name Vivian is "full of life" Vivian is used as both a boy's name, and as a girl's name.

Vivien

Pronunciation: VIV-e-en

Vivien is of Latin origin. The meaning of the name Vivien is "alive, lively". From the Roman family name Vivianus. Borne in Arthurian legend; Vivien was the Lady of the Lake and the mistress of Merlin. She stole Lancelot when he was a child and raised him herself.

Wallis
Pronunciation: WAL-is
The name Wallis if of Old English origin. The meaning of Wallis is "from Wales". Wallis is a variant of the name Wallace. The Duchess of Windsor, Wallis Simpson popularised the name.

Wanda
Pronunciation: WAHN-dah
The name Wanda is of Slavic origin. The meaning of Wanda is "the tribe of the Vandals". An ancient Slavonic tribe named The Vandals, were well known for their destructive behavior, which led to the modern term 'vandalism.' The name Wanda was popularised in Ouida's novel, Wanda (1883).

Wanetta
Pronunciation: WAN-ett-a
The name Wanetta is of Old English origin. The meaning of Wanetta is "pale-skinned".

Warda
Pronunciation: WAR-da
The name Warda is of Old German origin. The meaning of Warda is "Guardian".

Wava
Pronunciation: WAY-vah
The name Wava is of Slavic origin. The meaning of Wava is "stranger". Wave is a Russian form of the name Barbara.

Waverly
Pronunciation: WAY-ver-lee
The name Waverly is of Old English origin. The meaning of Waverly is "meadow of quivering aspens". Waverly is also a place name.

Wendell
Pronunciation: WEN-dell
The name Wendell is of Old German origin. The meaning of Wendell is "wanderer".

Wendy
Pronunciation: WEN-dee
Wendy is of English origin. The meaning of the name Wendy is "friend". The name was created by J M Barrie for the heroine of Peter Pan (1904). Wendy was a nickname which was given to him by a friend's daughter.

Weslee
Pronunciation: WEZ-lee
The name Weslee is of Old English origin. The meaning of Weslee is "western meadow". Weslee is a feminine form of the name Wesley.

Whitley
Pronunciation: WHIT-lee
The name Whitley is of Old English origin. The meaning of Whitley is "white meadow". Whitley is also a place name.

Whitney
Pronunciation: WHIT-nee
Whitney is of Old English origin. The meaning of the name Whitney is "white island". Whitney is also a place name. Originally used as a boy's name, Whitney became a popular first name for females in the early 1980's. American singer, Whitney

Houston (1963-2012) popularised the name.

Wilda
Pronunciation: WIL-da
The name Wilda is of Old English and Old German origin. The meaning of Wilda is "untamed".

Wilhelmina
Pronunciation: WIL-ah-men-ah
The name Wilhelmina is of Old German origin. The Meaning of Wilhelmina is "determined protector".

Willa
Pronunciation: WIL-ah
The name Willa is of Old German origin. The meaning of Willa is "determined protector". Willa is a feminine form of the name William.

Willow
Pronunciation: WIL-oh
The name Willow is of English origin. The meaning of Willow is "grace". Willow is the name of a species of tree, known for its grace.

Wilma
Pronunciation: WIL-ma
The name Wilma is of Old German origin. The meaning of Wilma is "determined protector". Wilma is a short form of the name Wilhelmina. The name became famous with Hanna-Barbera's cartoon serious, The Flintstones. Wilma Flintstone was a Stone Age housewife.

Wilona
Pronunciation: WIL-oo-na
The name Wilona is of Old English origin. The meaning of Wilona is "longed for".

Winifred
Pronunciation: WIN-a-fred
The name Winifred is of Old English and Welsh origin. The meaning of Winifred is "blessed, peace". Borne by a martyred Welsh Princess, Winifred was traditionally known as the patron saint of virgins.

Winona
Pronunciation: wyw-NOH-nah
The name Winona is of Native American Indian origin. The meaning of Winona is "eldest daughter". From Sioux Indian. The name was made famous by Hollywood actress Winona Ryder.

Winsome
Pronunciation: WIN-sum
The name Winsome is of Old English origin. The meaning Winsome is "agreeable".

Winter
Pronunciation: WIN-ter
The name Winter is of Old English origin. The meaning of Winter is unknown. Winter is also the name of one of the four seasons, Spring, Summer, Autumn, Winter.

Wren
Pronunciation: WREN

The name Wren is of Old English origin. The meaning of Wren is unknown. Wren is also the name of a small brown songbird.

Wyanet
Pronunciation: WHY-an-et
The name Wyanet is of Native American Indian origin. The meaning of Wyanet is "beautiful".

Wyetta
Pronunciation: WHY-ett-a
The name Wyetta is of Old English origin. The meaning of Wyetta is "war strength". Wyetta is a feminine form of the Old English name Wyatt.

Wynne
Pronunciation: WYN-ee
The name Wynne comes from the Welsh word, gwen, which means "fair, holy, blessed, white." The meaning of the name Wynne is "friend". Wynne is also a variant of the name Wynn. Wynne is used as both a girl's name, and as a boy's name.

Wyome
Pronunciation: WY-o-me
The name Wyome is of Native American Indian origin. The meaning of Wyome is "wide plain".

Xanthe
Pronunciation: ZAN-thah
The name Xanthe is of Greek origin. The meaning of Xanthe is "yellow, blonde". From Greek Xanthos.

Xaviera
Pronunciation: zay-vee-HER-ah
The name Xaviera is of Arabic and Basque origin. The meaning of the name Xaviera is "bright, splendid". The name is a feminine form of the masculine name, Xavier.

Xeni
Pronunciation: SHEH-nee
The name Xeni is of Guatemalan origin. The meaning of Xeni is "protector of plants". Derived from the name Xeniflóres.

Xenia
Pronunciation: ZAYN-yah
The name Xenia is of Greek origin. The meaning of the name Xenia is "hospitable".

Xylia
Pronunciation: ZYE-lee-ah
The name Xylia is of Greek origin. The meaning of Xylia is "woodland".

Y

Yaffa
Pronunciation: YA-ffa
The name Yaffa is of Hebrew origin. The meaning of Yaffa is "lovely".

Yakira
Pronunciation: ya-KEE-ra
The name Yakira is of Hebrew origin. The meaning of Yakira is "precious".

Yalena
Pronunciation: yal-EE-na
The name Yalena is of Greek and Russian origin. The meaning of Yalena is "sun ray". Yalena is a variant of the name Helen.

Yaminah
Pronunciation: yah-mi-NAH
The name Yaminah is of Arabic origin. The meaning of Yaminah is "suitable".

Yannick
Pronunciation: YANN-ick
Yannick if of French and Hebrew origin. The meaning of the name Yannick is "God is gracious". The name is used as both a boy's name, and as a girl's name. Yannick is variant of the name John.

Yara
Pronunciation: YAH-rah
The name Yara is of Brazilian and Arabic origin. The meaning of Yara is "small butterfly".

Yarina
Pronunciation: ya-RI-na
The name Yarina is of Russian origin. The meaning of Yarina is "peace". Yarina is a variant of the Greek name Irene.

Yarmila
Pronunciation: yar-MIL-LA
The name Yarmila is of Slavic origin. The meaning of Yarmila is "trader".

Yasmin, Yasmine
Pronunciation: yahz-MEEN
The name Yasmin is of Arabic and Persian origin. The meaning of Yasmin is "jasmine flower". The name is a variation of Jasmine.

Yesenia
Pronunciation: yeh-SEE-nee-ah
Yesenia is of Spanish origin. The meaning of Yesenia is unknown. Yesenia is variant of Llesenia.

Ynez
Pronunciation: ee-NEZ
The name Ynez is of French and Spanish origin. The meaning of Ynez is "chaste". Ynez is a variant of the Greek name Agnes.

Yoana
Pronunciation: yo-ANA
The name Yoana is of Hebrew origin. The meaning of Yoana is "God is gracious". The name is a variant of Joanna and a feminine form of the masculine name John.

Yoko
Pronunciation: YO-ko
The name Yoko is of Japanese origin. The meaning of Yōko is "good, positive".

Yolanda
Pronunciation: yoh-LAHN-dah
Yolanda is of Greek and Spanish origin. The meaning of the name Yolanda is "violet flower".

Yolande
Pronunciation: yoh-LAHN-dee
The name Yolande is of Latin origin. The meaning of Yolande is "violet flower". A variation of the French name Iolanthe derived from the Italian name Violanta.

Yonina
Pronunciation: yo-ni-NA
The name Yonina is of Hebrew origin. The meaning of Yonina is "dove".

Yosepha
Pronunciation: yo-se-pha
The name Yosepha is of Hebrew origin. The meaning of Yosepha is "Jehovah increases". The name is a Feminine form of the name Joseph.

Yseult
Pronunciation: yse-(u)-lt
The name Yseult is of French origin. The meaning of Yseult is "fair lady". The name is also a variant of the name Isolde.

Yudit
Pronunciation: YU-dit
The name Yudit is of Hebrew origin. The meaning of Yudit is "praise".

Yuliya
Pronunciation: yu-li-ya
The name Yuliya is of Russian origin. The meaning of Yuliya is "youthful". The name is a variant of Julia.

Yumiko
Pronunciation: yoo-mee-koh
Yumiko is of Japanese origin. The meaning of the name Yumiko is "arrow child".

Yuriko
Pronunciation: yoo-ree-koh
The name Yuriko is of Japanese origin. The meaning of Yuriko is "lily child".

Yvette
Pronunciation: ee-VET
The name Yvette is of French origin. The meaning of Yvette is "yew". The name is a feminine form of the French name Yves.

Yvonne
Pronunciation: ee-VAHN
The name Yvonne is of French and Old German origin. The meaning of Yvonne is "yew". A feminine form of the French name Yves.

Z

Zahavah
Pronunciation: ZA-hav-AH
The name Zahavah is of Hebrew origin. The meaning of Zahavah is "gilded".

Zaida
Pronunciation: ZAY-dah
The name Zaida is of Arabic origin. The meaning of Zaida is "prosperous".

Zaina
Pronunciation: ZAY-nah
Zaina is of Greek origin. The meaning of the name Zaina is "beauty". Zaina is a variant of the name Xenia.

Zalika
Pronunciation: za-LEE-kah
The name Zalika is of Swahili origin. The meaning of Zalika is "well born".

Zandra
Pronunciation: ZAHN-dra
The name Zandra is of Spanish origin. The meaning of Zandra is "man's defender". Zandra is a diminutive of the Greek name Alexandra.

Zaneta
Pronunciation: zah-NEE-tah
The name Zaneta is of Spanish origin. The meaning of Zaneta is unknown. Borne by a saint.

Zara
Pronunciation: ZR-ah
The name Zara is of Arabic origin. The meaning of Zara is "radiance". The name is possibly taken from the Hebrew meaning, 'bright as the dawn'. Zara is a diminutive of the name Sarah.

Zarina
Pronunciation: za-REEN-ah
Zarina is of Persian origin. The meaning of the name Zarina is "golden".

Zea
Pronunciation: ZEE-a
The name Zea is of Latin origin. The meaning of Zea is "grain".

Zarya
Pronunciation: ZAR-ya
The name Zarya is of Slavic origin. The meaning of Zarya is "protector of warriors". Borne in mythology, Zarya is a water priestess and protector of the warriors.

Zefira
Pronunciation: ZE-fir-a
The name Zefira is of Hebrew origin. The meaning of Zefira is "morning".

Zelda
Pronunciation: ZEH-dah
Zelda is of Old German origin. The meaning of the name Zelda is "dark battle". Originally used as a nickname of the Old German name, Griselda.

Zelenia
Pronunciation: ZEL-een-ia
The name Zelenia is of Greek origin. The meaning of Zelenia is "the moon". Zelenia is a variant of the Greek name Selena.

Zena
Pronunciation: ZEE-na
The name Zena is of Greek origin. The meaning of Zena is "guest, stranger". The name is a variant of Xenia.

Zelma
Pronunciation: ZEL-mah
The name Zelma is of Old German origin. The meaning of Zelma is "helmet of God". Zelma is a variant of the name Selma.

Zenobia
Pronunciation: ze-NOH-bee-ah
Zenobia is of Greek origin. The meaning of the name Zenobia is "life of Zeus". Borne by a 3rd-century queen of Palmyra in the Arabian desert. The name was revived in the 19th century.

Zetta
Pronunciation: ZEE-ta
The name Zetta is of Hebrew origin. The meaning of Zetta is "olive".

Zoe
Pronunciation: ZOH-ee
Zoe is of Greek origin. The meaning of the name Zoe is "life". Originally a Greek Jewish translation of the Hebrew name, Eve, meaning 'life.' The name was borne by a 3rd-century Roman martyr. The name was adopted in Britain in the 19th century; the name has been in regular use since.

Zola
Pronunciation: ZO-la
The name Zola is of Italian origin. The meaning of Zola is "lump of earth". The name is possibly a variation of the Greek name Zoe. Zola was adopted as a first name in the late 20th century.

Zora
Pronunciation: ZOR-ah
The name Zora is of Slavic origin. The meaning of Zora is "dawn". Variation: Zorah.

Banned baby names around the world

Although the UK and the USA have some of the most liberal rules in the world when it comes to baby names, other countries have created lists of banned names that you cannot name your child in their country.

The Girl Baby Names for 2017 book has put together some of the funniest and most bizarre banned baby names from around the world.

Mexico

The Mexican State of Sonora released a long list of names that are banned for reasons being that they are 'derogatory, pejorative, discriminatory or for simply lacking in meaning.' The list of prohibited names in Sonora include;

All Power	Petronilo
Batman	Pocahontas
Burger King	Privado
Cesárea	Rambo
Christmas Day	Robocop
Circuncisión	Rocky
Email	Rolling Stone
Espinacia	Terminator
Facebook	Sonora querida
Harry Potter	Telesforo
Hermione	Tránsito
Hitler	Twitter
Iluminada	Usnavy

James Bond	Virgen
Lady Di	Verulo
Masiosare	Yahoo
Micheline	Zoila Rosa

Saudi Arabia

Saudi Arabia released their list of banned baby names which include any names that have royal connotations such as prince or princess, names of prophets, western names are also included in the list. The list of forbidden baby names in Saudi Arabia include;

Abdul Naser	Loland
Al Mamlaka (The Kingdom)	Malaak (Angel)
Alice	Malika (Queen)
Amir (Prince)	Maline
Aram	Maya
Basmala (utterance of the name of God)	Nabi (Prophet)
Barrah	Nabiyya (Female Prophet)
Baseel	Nardeen
Bayan	Naris
Binyamin (Arabic for Benjamin)	Randa
Elaine	Rital
Iman	Rama (Hindu God)
Inar	Sandy

Jibreel (Angel Gabriel)	Sumuw (Highness)
Kibrial	Tabarak (Blessed)
Lareen	Tilaj
Lauren	Yara
Linda	Wireelam

Australia

Australian government has 'proposed names will not be registered if they are obscene or offensive, unreasonably long, contain symbols without phonetic significance or are not in the public interest for some other reason.' Some of the baby names banned in Australia include the following;

Batman	Maryjuana
Bonghead	Medicare
(Blankspace)	Ned Kelly
Chief Maximus	Osama
Circumcision	Panties
Chow Tow	Pieandsauce
Dick Head	Post Master General
G-Bang	President
Goose	#ROFL
Hitler	Ranga
Ice-T	Scrotum

Ikea	Shithead
iMac	Spinach
Jesus Christ	Smelly
Lol	Snort
Lucifer	Virgin
Martian	

Germany

German guidelines state that names must indicate the gender of the child and must not be likely to lead to humiliation. You are forbidden to use surnames or the names of objects or products as first names. In order to protect the child, the name must not be absurd or degrading in any way. Local registrars decide which names to approve and which ones to reject.

A Turkish couple who were living in Germany were refused the permission to call the child Osama Bin Laden. Gender Neutral names are also rejected such as the name Matti.

Amongst some of the banned baby names in Germany are;

Agfa	Osama Bin Laden
Atom Fired	Pillula
Gramopho	Puhbert
Bierstübl	Satan
Cain	Schnucki
Hitler	Schroeder
Judas	Sputnik

Lenin	Stompie
MC Donald	Troublemaker
Ogino	The number 'Pi'
Omo	Woodstock

China

In China, a couple tried to name their child Wang @. The symbol in Chinese is pronounced "ai-ta", which means "Love him." The parents claimed that the @ symbol echoed the love that they had for the child.

Malaysia

Malaysian authorities have also banned the use of numbers in baby names, Japanese car names and royal titles. A list of banned baby names has been published. Included on the list is the Canonese monikers Sor Chai which means Insane, Chow Tow, meaning Smelly Head. The use of Woti has also been discouraged as a baby name as it means sexual intercourse.

New Zealand

A court in New Zealand took over the guardianship of a young girl named, Talula Does The Hula From Hawaii so that they could change her name. The judge condemned the name and the rising trend of parents using wacky baby names, claiming that it would lead to bullying.

Another couple in New Zealand were banned from naming their twins Fish and Chips, although the name Number 16 Bus Shelter was approved by authorities.

Names on the list of banned baby names in New Zealand include;

Anal	Majesty
Baron	Major
Bishop	Messiah

Duke	President
Judge	Prince
King	Princess
Knight	Queen
Lady	Royale
Lucifer	

Portugal

Portugal has put a ban on parents using nicknames on their childs birth certificates. This means the name Tom would be rejected however the full name Thomas would be accepted.

Amongst the banned names in Portugal are;

Albuquerque
Ashanti
Ben-Hur
Brilhante
Britta Nórdica
Do Sorriso
Faruk
Mar E Sol (Portuguese for sean & sun)
Nazareth Fernades

Nirvana
Olaf
Portugal
Sandokan
Satélite
Sayonara (Japanese for goodbye)
Viking
Zingara (Italian for gypsy)

BIBLOGRAPHY

Cresswell, Julia
Bloomsbury Dictionary of First Names
Bloomsbury, London, 1992

Cross. F. L and Livingstone E A, ed
Oxford Dictionary of the Christian Church
Oxford University Press, 1997

Drunkling, Leslie
First names first
J M Dent & Sons Ltd, London 1977

Fergusson, Rosalind
Choose Your Baby's name
Penguin, London 1987

Hall, James
Dictionary of Subjects and Symbols in Art
John Murrary, 1992

Hanks, Patrick and Falvia Hodges
A Concise Dictionary of First Names
Oxford University Press, Oxford, 1997

Holy Bible
Cambridge University Press

Macleod, Iseabail and Terry Freedman
The Wordsworth Dictionary of First Names

Wordsworth Editions Limited, London, 1995

Office for National Statistics

Baby Names, England and Wales

Publish 2014

Pickering, David

The Penguin Dictionary of First Names

Penguin, 2004

Room, Adrian

Brewer's Names

Cassell, London, 1992

Stafford, Diane

The Big Book of 60, 000 Baby Names

Sourcebooks, Inc, 2006

Strong, James

Strong's Concordance of the Bible

Thomas Nelson 1980

Withycombe, E G

Oxford Dictionary of English Christian Names

Oxford University Press, Oxford 1977

Made in the USA
Lexington, KY
10 December 2017